KEN REXFORD

JEBIDDING

T BRIDGE

MODERN APPROACH

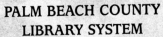
R POINT PRESS | TORONTO

Master Point Press
331 Douglas Ave.
Toronto, Ontario, Canada
M5M 1H2
(416) 781-0351
Website: http://www.masterpointpress.com
Email: info@masterpointpress.com

Library and Archives Canada Cataloguing in Publication

Rexford, Ken
    Cuebidding at bridge : a modern approach / written by Ken Rexford.

ISBN-13: 978-1-897106-17-4
ISBN-10: 1-897106-17-3

1. Contract bridge--Bidding. I. Title.

GV1282.4.R49 2006   795.41'52   C2006-904820-7

Editor   Ray Lee
Interior format   Suzanne Hocking
Cover and interior design   Olena S. Sullivan/New Mediatrix
Photo credit: Michael Blann/DigitalVision/Getty Images

Printed in Canada by Webcom Inc.

1 2 3 4 5 6 7   10 09 08 07 06

TABLE OF CONTENTS

FOREWORD

In the nearly 17 years that I have been employed by the ACBL, I have spent considerable time reading bridge books. Until now, it was work — I read the books for the purpose of reviewing them in the *Bridge Bulletin*, the magazine of which I am editor. It feels strange to be writing about a book without that critical eye, but here goes.

Not long ago, I had occasion to review some old copies of the television show, *Championship Bridge*. The best and brightest of the bridge world at the time — the early Sixties — were featured. What sticks with me as I reflect on those shows is the lousy bidding. The rankest of today's newcomers would bid rings around the experts who appeared on *Championship Bridge*.

Anyone who plays tournament bridge today has benefited from all the advances in bidding that have taken place in the 40-plus years since that show first aired. Many outstanding bidding theorists have produced huge improvements in the language of partner communication.

The book you are about to read may not advance bidding theory in quantum leaps, but the topic of cuebids is as important as it is misunderstood. If your partnership's slam explorations consist of Blackwood only and you're happy with that, this might not be the book for you. On the other hand, if you're not satisfied with your results in that area, I encourage you to have a closer look.

This is an exhaustive work, covering a lot of territory. You might not agree with everything you read — and it would be a mammoth undertaking to try to adopt it all — but it will get you thinking about your bidding and offer many ways to improve it. After all, bridge is the ultimate game for thinkers.

Brent Manley
March 2006

INTRODUCTION

At the 2005 Pittsburgh Nationals, I had the honor of playing against the Pavlicek team in the first round of the Vanderbilt. Although my team lost miserably, one deal piqued my interest. Our opponents missed a grand slam in a cuebidding sequence that featured a rather interesting post-auction alert. Apparently a bid of 5♠ during the auction had been meant as a desperate attempt to get out at 5NT, and further to imply, 'Partner, I am lost in the auction.'

Later that week, I witnessed Zia Mahmood and Michael Rosenberg miss another grand slam, also as a result of what appeared to be either a cuebidding sequence that had gone off the rails or an auction where the pair lacked the specific tools to explore for this particular slam.

The fact that expert pairs were having trouble communicating in certain slam sequences intrigued me, and I began asking around about the meaning of certain cuebids in the specific sequences faced by these players. I received varying answers, but no one seemed to know for sure.

When I set out to write this book, the motivation was not truly to re-invent the wheel, but perhaps that was, in a sense, the result. I researched multiple sources for clues as to what 'Italian-Style Cuebidding' means. (By 'Italian', I mean that approach to cuebidding that has its origins in the theory of the Italian Blue Teams of World Championship fame.) The works of Giorgio Belladonna, including *Cuebidding to Slam*, coauthored by Claudio

Petroncini, published in 1990 and translated by Daniel Neill of Kentucky in 2004, served as a starting point, perhaps reflecting the 'old school' theories of the originators. For the 'modern' perspective, I reviewed a series of three articles by Fred Gitelman, "Improving 2/1 Game Force", published originally in *Canadian Master Point* magazine.

Neither of these two texts showed me a functional wheel and the theories were at points inconsistent with each other. In short, it was a mess. Just look over Vugraph Archives to see for yourself. The professionals might all agree what to open, what to respond and what to rebid, but their cuebidding sequences diverge on to all sorts of strange paths.

I delved deeper, reading brief notes in bridge books, reviewing system notes for many of the great players and conducting online research. My online studies referenced numerous lesson notes, commentaries and the like. I even posed questions on bridge forums for the masses to respond to. Finally, I turned to professional friends of mine, discussing the issue between rounds over cigarettes. My major source here was my friend Kenneth Eichenbaum of Columbus, Ohio.

The result was a mismatched collection of majority views, minority views, insane views and sometimes no opinions or views at all. Next I used logic, and sometimes personal preference, to produce a perspective that seemed consistent with the rest of the theory.

After much study, I started to recognize three critical concepts:

1. There are some hand types that can be specifically categorized as lending themselves to certain 'follow-up' cuebidding sequences.
2. Even expert pairs lack agreements on the meaning of some cuebidding sequences. They rely on 'inspired' inferential cuebids and the hope that partner is on the same page. Without agreed principles to ensure that the partnership is at least working from the same book, this is unacceptable.
3. Although there is no complete set of cuebidding rules available, some sort of handbook must, in theory, exist. (A good friend and partner calls this the 'black hole' theory: 'I cannot see it, but I know it is there.')

With all this in mind, I decided to put together a disciplined approach, admittedly incorporating some new ideas. I decided to boldly go where no human had gone before. What I have attempted in this book is, in part, to isolate certain hand types and to set up predetermined meanings for cuebids in the context of a given auction. I have also tried to establish consistent principles to enable partnerships actually to be on the same page, and to know that they are supported when heading into uncharted waters.

I understand in advance that some of my theories may have flaws. I also understand in advance that, although many of my applications are practical and fairly easy to use, some of them will seem esoteric to many players. Furthermore, even if one was to assume that my applications are all sound, there is a tremendous amount of memory work and thought involved. Many of these bids are not for the casual partnership.

However, my main goal in writing this book is to enlighten, not necessarily to pronounce the definitive answer to cuebidding in slam auctions. I hope to lay the groundwork for things to come. With any luck, my ideas will inspire others to discuss, modify and change our concepts of cuebidding.

The theories I put forward, then, are a melting pot, based on logic and consistency, and unified by my personal perspective. That may frighten some who know me, but I believe that with a great deal of guidance I may have approached the Tao of cuebidding.

My approach to writing this book was to start with a simple auction: a major is agreed as trumps, in a 2/1 game-forcing auction, at the two-level. A whole world of space exists in which to describe one's hand. Conventional wisdom seemed to support treating calls below three of an agreed major as shape bids. I rejected this approach; it seemed unnecessary and redundant, especially when I thought through the alternative I ended up adopting.

Next, I assumed a principle: jumps, which consume space, should be well defined. At the same time, failing to jump should rule out possession of a hand appropriate for a jump. This concept leads to interesting inferences, which to my knowledge have never been truly explored before now. I also developed methods for handling the next call after a jump in a cuebidding sequence.

Finally, I examined how the structure is affected if suit agreement occurs at the three-level, or if the opponents intervene, and investigated the special requirements of auctions involving minor suits.

It occurred to me as I wrote all of this down that many people do not grasp the whole concept of cuebidding. The extreme cuebidding novice thinks that cuebidding is merely an alternative to Blackwood and hence useless. Admittedly, if cuebidding were only a means of asking for aces, it would be of rare utility. Traditional American cuebidding suffers from this misconception, at least as practiced by most.

You have advanced a tad in cuebidding sophistication if you realize that one of the key purposes of cuebidding is to avoid bidding a slam off two quick losers in the same suit. Cuebidding, especially Italian-style, where first- and second-round controls are bid without priority, eliminates the unfortunate situation where we hold 33 HCP but are missing a cashing ace-king. But this is just one example of its usefulness.

Cuebidding is also a tool to spot the fit of the hand, as opposed to the fit of the trump suit only. To illustrate, consider this hand:

♠ A J 9 5 4   ♡ A Q J 4 2   ◇ 10 9   ♣ 8

If partner holds the K-Q-10-2 of spades, you have a great spade fit. Give him about 20 HCP and slam should be laydown, right?

Well, consider two possible hands for partner, each with the same spade holding. Opposite

♠ K Q 10 2   ♡ K 9   ◇ A K 5 4 3   ♣ A J

a 20-point hand, a grand slam is just about laydown. However, opposite

♠ K Q 10 2   ♡ K 9   ◇ Q J 5   ♣ A K Q J

a 21-HCP hand, the small slam will probably be set at Trick 2.

Taking this a step further, imagine partner has a hand like:

♠ K Q 10 2   ♡ K 9   ◇ A 3   ♣ 6 5 4 3 2

With that 'mere' 12-count, the small slam is easy, despite 'only' 24 HCP combined. Cuebidding, properly handled, should make it easy for a pair to bid to slam on these hands or to stop safely before getting there. This is what cuebidding is all about.

THE BASIC RULES OF ITALIAN-STYLE CUEBIDDING

The art of cuebidding is best explored in the context of ideal situations. When the auction is contested, or the cuebidding starts at a higher level, general rules from the ideal situation still apply. However, both the limitations of the auction and the special concerns of competitive auctions each create exceptions to those rules. Therefore, it seems logical to start a discussion of cuebidding theory from the point of view of an ideal auction.

One of the difficulties that I faced while writing this book was that cuebidding theory is so strongly contextual. As a simple example of what I mean, consider a bid of 4♣. If you were to ask someone what 4♣ means, they would assume that 4♣ was the opening bid. If you then said, "No, a 4♣ bid in the middle of a complicated and contested auction," no answer would be possible. Context is required.

The context of any bid depends upon several factors. First, the context is defined by the general systemic approach. Second, context is defined by the calls within that general systemic approach that preceded the 4♣ bid. Third, context includes, necessarily, partnership agreements and definitions. Context may even include opposition bidding and the varying definitions provided for their bidding. Thus, the meaning of a 4♣ bid is dependent upon all of these factors.

If, after review of all of these factors, 4♣ happens to be a cuebid, then it says something about clubs — probably. However, what message that bid sends depends on not only the context, but also the necessities of the predicted auction. In other words, 4♣ sends a message relevant to a hypothetical slam that we are exploring and describes a holding that is in some way helpful to achieving that goal.

Throughout this book, I'm going to assume in many places that the contextual system is one where a two-level response to a one-level opening is forcing to game. This would typically be part of the 2/1 Game Force system, although several other systems feature a similar approach. One of the benefits to this is that it facilitates cuebidding sequences at low levels in many auctions. Additionally, I have assumed a general set of conventions that are fairly typical, although I do propose the use of a few that are rarely seen.

I have done this because I need a context within which to discuss the principles and theory of cuebidding. Without the context of a systemic approach and assumed conventions, defining a specific cuebid in my approach is as impossible as defining what 4♣ means without an auction. This reality may explain why so few prior attempts have been made to discuss cuebidding theory as a whole.

This overall context is going to generate some extra work for those readers who use different systemic approaches. You will be assumed to understand the general 2/1 Game Force system. You will then read about cuebidding in that context. From that study, you will learn principles. Then, the hard part! You will need to discuss with your partner whatever adjustments to the proposed approach are necessary if the structure is to fit within your own system.

The challenge, however, will not be as difficult as you may initially expect. The style of cuebidding I describe is not truly a set of defined bids. This is not like learning the various responses to Roman Keycard Blackwood and the possible continuations. Rather, cuebidding has basic rules that are applied logically to each unique situation. If you understand the principles, you can figure out the meaning of cuebids at the table in a completely undiscussed auction.

Even if your systemic approach is identical to mine, the pages that follow will not cover every conceivable auction. However, I believe that if you use the tools provided, you and your partner will end up on the same page if one of you tosses out a strange, undiscussed call. The idea is not that our hypothetical 4♣ call be defined for all possible auctions; rather, the meaning of 4♣ should be clear so long as the principles are mutually understood and applied in the new auction — your own auction, not one defined by my systemic preference.

The most economical auction for cuebidding purposes is one where the partnership, unimpeded, using 2/1 GF as the general approach, agrees a major at the two-level, after each partner has shown a second side suit. For example:

WEST	EAST
1♡	2♣
2◇	2♡
?	

As this is the ideal auction type, this is where I propose to start. We have agreed our suit at the two-level, and the opponents have been kind enough to stay out of our way. We have forced to game, and everything we bid from here on will be regarded as some kind of move towards slam, if it is not recognizably a sign-off. We can discuss the cuebidding structure from here and later introduce modifications for the difficult scenarios — for example, where suit agreement takes more space or the opponents intervene.

Italian-style cuebidding can be described simplistically as cuebidding 'values', with each bid described by a general set of principles. Exactly what values are shown will depend on whether or not the suit is one we have bid, and which of us bid it. Bypassing a cuebid usually denies the ability to make that bid, while a jump to game says that a hole shown by partner cannot be filled. These principles will be explained in more detail in the next chapter.

In addition, there are certain treatments that I recommend incorporating in the slam approach structure, including Serious 3NT, Last Train, and using 2NT where available as a way to distinguish between hands with and without strong trumps.

Finally, I have assigned very specific meanings to jumps in a cuebidding sequence ('Picture Jumps'); these too will be described later in the book. I am going to explain how one should think about these auctions and I will even suggest a few more useful agreements and treatments.

How all these ideas fit together into a coherent package is my main theme. It is, however, important to recognize that everything does fit together. It is critical that the partnership adopt an inclusive approach to cuebidding. All facets of cuebidding play off one another. If the partnership adopts Serious 3NT, then a 4♣ cuebid made instead of and bypassing 3NT takes on new meaning: it now shows weakness. If one adopts Last Train, the last cuebid below game is not necessarily legitimate. If one uses

2NT to show poor trumps, then a cuebid that bypasses 2NT shows good trumps. If one uses Picture Jumps, cuebidding without jumps denies certain holdings.

The total approach I describe employs a number of tools. Take one out and the structure changes. I suggest using everything I propose, unless you are ready to work through the implications of not using a tool and adjust your thinking accordingly.

Underlying all of this is the principle that cuebidding is an 'approach art'. What this means is that each player, back and forth, normally makes the cheapest informative call available. Jumping around is discouraged and, accordingly, shows specific holdings. The 'normal' sequence involves a series of back-and-forth bids, where each person shows what he has up-the-line.

Within this context, 'captaincy' is often unresolved for a long time. Captaincy is a concept where one partner, perhaps deemed to have superior informational advantage as a starting point, could be viewed as a person asking questions, with the other player answering. Cuebidding, in contrast, is often like tossing a hot rock back and forth.

Imagine a typical auction, with comments rather than bids:

Opener:	'I have spades and an opener.'
Responder:	'I have diamonds and an opener also.'
Opener:	'I have hearts, too.'
Responder:	'Let's agree on spades.'
Opener:	'Yeah, but my spades are lousy.'
Responder:	'I like my diamonds, but I have nothing in clubs to stop them from cashing two tricks.'
Opener:	'I like my hearts. Plus, don't you worry about clubs.'
Responder:	'My spades are great.'
Opener:	'Well, now I'm really thinking about slam.'
Responder:	'I have third-round club control, if you care.'
Opener:	'That may help, but I'm still not sure. I have a diamond card for you, though.'
Responder:	'Well, if you're serious about slam and have that diamond king I was wondering about, then we must be real close here. I'm giving it a go!'

Wouldn't it be nice to bid this way? Simply state what you mean...

Context — The Bigger Picture

Cuebidding is enhanced not only by what is bid, but also inferentially by what is not bid, and even on occasion by what has not yet been bid.

As a simple example, if you could have bid 4♣, but instead you bid 4◊, you are directly showing an important diamond feature. You also normally imply the lack of an important club feature. However, a 4◊ bid might actually imply a club control if it were made by a person whose partner had already denied a club control necessary for a slam to succeed. It might even imply a necessary heart feature, for the same reason.

This idea can be restated. Consider an auction where one player has denied first- or second-round control in either diamonds or hearts, with spades agreed as trumps in a game-forcing auction. Suppose the player's partner is in a position to make a cuebid of 4◊ or 4♡. Obviously, he would not cuebid if slam was definitely not there (i.e. if he knew there were two quick losers in one suit). Therefore, if either diamonds or hearts were wide open, he would sign off, right? Inferentially, then, a cuebid of 4◊ would directly show a control in diamonds and, logically, a control in hearts as well. In the same way, a cuebid of 4♡ would directly show a control in hearts and also imply a control in diamonds. Thus, a principle arises. Actual cuebids send positive messages about the suit actually bid. Furthermore, as cuebids are made for a purpose, cuebids also imply possession of any necessary control that has been denied by partner. This inferential control could be a bypassed suit (diamonds in the example of the 4♡ cuebid) or a 'future' suit (hearts in the example of the 4◊ cuebid).

How does this principle work in the real world? Suppose you are dealt this hand:

♠ A K 4 3 2   ♡ A 2   ◊ K Q 4 2   ♣ Q 8

You open 1♠ and partner responds 2♣. You rebid 2◊ and partner agrees spades, bidding 2♠. You then cuebid 3♣, showing one of the top three club honors and good trumps (trust me for now). Partner cuebids 3♠, showing the missing spade honor, but denying the diamond ace while also denying a heart control. Think through the two options of a 4◊ cuebid and a 4♡ cuebid.

WEST	EAST
1♠	2♣
2♢	2♠
3♣	3♠
4♢/4♡	

If you cuebid 4♢, this shows (again, trust me) two top diamond honors. If you did not have a heart control, you would simply sign off in 4♠. Slam would be hopeless. Thus 4♢ guarantees to partner that you also have a heart control. Why? Because bidding is more than an exercise in hearing the sound of your own voice.

What about bidding 4♡ instead? A 4♡ bid, out of context, merely shows a heart control and denies two top diamond honors. However, it also implies, very strongly, a diamond control. With a queen-top diamond suit, slam would have been ruled out, unless partner holds a singleton in diamonds (impossible, for he would have splintered, considering the rest of his known hand) or a void in diamonds (in which case he may continue on, notwithstanding your signoff suggestion).

Additionally, either call suggests first-round control of one of the red suits and at least second-round control of the other; otherwise, two red aces would cash. All of these 'meanings' are logical inferences.

Cuebids are also defined *in context*, that is, by prior actions and by prior alternatives that were not selected. If, for example, you previously denied a club control, all future calls also deny a club control. Hence, a cuebid of clubs after denying a club control shows a lesser club feature, perhaps the queen or a doubleton or the jack, whatever seems contextually most relevant and/or possible. Similarly, if you could have made a splinter previously, a cuebidding sequence without the splinter suggests a holding unsuitable for a splinter.

True understanding of a cuebidding sequence, therefore, requires an understanding of the inferences involved. This includes understanding the meaning of alternatives to the 'simple' cuebidding sequence, in particular the use of jumps in a cuebidding sequence. Jumps, because they consume vast amounts of potential bidding space, should be well-defined bids. Therefore, non-jump sequences should derive body and meaning from the failure to use the jump alternative.

Do you see the 'trick' to cuebidding? It would be ridiculous to try to imagine every auction, even without interference, and proceed to define every possible bid. Even if you could do that, no one I know could memorize it all. The key to superior cuebidding is to learn the principles. Once you understand the principles, you will be able to figure out each new situation as it arises at the table. Sure, a precise definition exists for every bid, but only the bridge gods know exactly what they are. We mortals must figure it out each time anew. This is not impossible, but it can be difficult. On occasion, you will sit at the table looking dumb for a few seconds, but it is better to look dumb for a moment in the auction than to look dumb during the entire play of the hand!

- 2 -

CUEBIDDING WITHOUT JUMPS

As I mentioned earlier, cuebidding theory relies on inferences. Any theory that suffers from redundancies is poor theory — we need to make optimal use of the small number of auctions available to us, while minimizing or eliminating ambiguities. Thus, if we define strict parameters for jump auctions, then auctions where we fail to jump become narrower in scope. For now, however, let's explore some of the basic concepts without worrying about exactly what the jump bids mean.

GENERAL PRINCIPLES

The general rules for the first round of cuebidding, by which I mean the first opportunity to cuebid a suit, are as follows:

1. *Cuebids of a side suit belonging to the cuebidder show two of the top three honors.*

WEST	EAST
1♠	2♣
2♦	2♠
3♦	

Bidding 3♦, West confirms two of the top three diamond honors (there are other inferences, but let's not worry about those for now). Notice that according to our structure, this call does not show any extra length in diamonds — it is unambiguously a cuebid.

2. *Cuebids of a side suit belonging to partner show one of the top three honors.*

West	East
1♠	2♣
2♦	2♠
3♣	

Here, West confirms possession of one of the top three club honors.

3. *2NT as a cuebid denies good trumps (denies two of the top three honors).*

West	East
1♠	2♣
2♦	2♠
2NT	

In this auction, it is clear we have a fit and that 2NT is our trump denial. You should, however, make sure that you and your partner identify any auctions where you want to retain a natural 2NT call as an option.

4. *Bypassing 2NT as a cuebid promises good trumps.*

West	East
1♠	2♣
2♦	2♠
3♣	

Back to our previous auction, but now we know that West not only has a club honor, but also two of the top three spade honors (since he failed to bid 2NT).

5. *A cuebid of trumps (yes, this is possible) shows two of the top three honors, or the missing top honor if partner has already shown the other two top honors.*

West	East
1♠	2♣
2♦	2♠
3♣	3♠

East shows the remaining top trump honor, West having promised two already when he bypassed 2NT.

6. *Cuebids of unbid suits show first- or second-round control, in the form of honors (ace or king) or shortness (voids or singletons).*

West	East
1♠	2♣
2♦	2♠
3♣	3♡

East shows a heart control of some kind. One of the Italian innovations was to discard the traditional 'aces-first' cuebidding method. A sufficiency of first-round controls can be confirmed later in the auction if necessary.

7. *Bypassing a cuebid denies the ability to make that cuebid.*

West	East
1♠	2♣
2♦	2♠
3♦	

We're back to our first example auction, but now we know that West has (a) two of the top three trump honors (b) two of the top three diamond honors (c) none of the top three club honors, since he bypassed 3♣.

8. Bidding 3NT shows contextually serious slam interest.

This is an easy statement to make, but there are definitely auctions, even major-suit auctions, where you may want to offer 3NT as a place to play. For example, in 2/1,

West	East
1♡	2◇
2♡	3♡
3NT	

is a sequence where a natural meaning for 3NT can be useful. If you are going to play Serious 3NT, you need to have clear agreements with partner as to when 3NT is 'Serious' and when it is an offer to play there. For example, when a nine-card fit is known, or when both players have made cuebids, a 3NT bid should probably be Serious. Such discussion is beyond the scope of this book, but the rules do have to be established.

We shall explore the meaning of the phrase 'contextually serious' in later chapters; suffice it to say here that it means "serious in the light of whatever limits the auction has already placed on the 3NT bidder's hand".

9. Bypassing 3NT denies contextually serious slam interest.

West	East
1♡	2◇
2♡	3♡
4♣	

West denies a spade control (bypassing 3♠) and shows a club control. However, by failing to bid 3NT, he also expresses the view that his hand is poor for his bidding so far.

10. *The last possible cuebid below game in our suit is potentially artificial, a 'Last Train to Clarksville' cuebid, imprecisely showing continuing slam interest, with insufficient information to commit to the slam or to RKCB.*

A Last Train bid is hard to define, but you will probably know one when you see it. Basically, in some complex or crowded auctions, which we shall encounter in later chapters, the last available bid before game can become an all-purpose slam try, generally encouraging partner to continue, but not carrying a specific meaning in relation to the suit bid.

All this information can be refined later in the auction.

Secondary cuebids clarify and bolster; they add to the information provided by the primary cuebid. For example, cuebidding a suit after denying a control there shows tertiary values, like the queen or a doubleton. Cuebidding a suit after showing values in it shows extra honors or better shape. The specific meaning of a repeated cuebid has to be deduced from the context of the auction.

This 'statement' of theory is completely miserable, I realize, in explaining what I am getting at. Some further examples will best clarify what I mean.

Assume that an auction begins as follows:

WEST	EAST
1♠	2♣ (GF)
2♦	2♠
?	

What do we know so far?

Opener has announced possession of at least five spades and at least four diamonds, with his diamond suit likely to be decent, meaning at least Q-x-x-x. He will not have equal length in diamonds and clubs, because he did not raise clubs.

Responder has spade support, with a club suit. This could possibly be a three-card club suit, as a convenience bid on a flat hand.

Opener now bids 3♣. This provides a world of information. The simple general rule says that opener has a club honor, at least the queen. The simple inference of bypassing 2NT also confirms that opener has good trumps (two of the top three).

WEST	EAST
1♠	2♣
2♦	2♠
3♣	3♦

Responder now bids 3◊. Directly, we know responder has a top honor (ace or king or queen) in diamonds (one of opener's known long suits).

WEST	EAST
1♠	2♣
2♦	2♠
3♣	3♦
4♦	

Opener continues with 4◊. Directly, we know that opener has two of the top three honors in diamonds. As a simple inference from bypassed options, we also know that opener lacks a third top spade honor (he did not cuebid 3♠), lacks a heart control (he did not cuebid 3♡) and lacks serious slam interest (he did not cuebid 3NT).

The auction so far:

WEST	EAST
1♠	2♣
2♦	2♠
3♣	3♦
4♦	?

Let's end this example by assuming that although East has a promising hand, it does not include a heart control. Knowing his partner can't provide one either, East will simply sign off in 4♠ and the auction will end there.

Do you see now what I mean by contextual analysis? Each step of the cuebidding sequence has a context. The cuebid itself mentions only one detail directly, that the player has a value in the denomination named. However, the cuebid also relays other information via various logical inferences. These include inferences from bypassed cuebids, inferences from the sequence selected, inferences from partner's natural calls and the like.

Another example: again, a major is agreed at the two-level.

WEST	EAST
1♠	2♦
2♥	2♠
3♦	?

Opener has directly promised nothing more than the possession of one of the top three diamond honors. Inferentially, however, because of bypassed options, he is also showing two of the top three spade honors (he bypassed 2NT) and denying a first- or second-round club control, either shortness or an honor. Hence, opener must have at least two clubs. Notice that cuebidding sequences often carry messages about hand pattern.

Suppose responder now bids 3♠. The direct meaning is that responder also has good trumps. Usually, this would show two of the top three trump honors, but opener has already promised two of these honors by failing to bid 2NT. Hence, responder has the one missing spade honor.

Inferentially, responder was also unable to make a 3♥ call, meaning that he lacks a control in hearts, a suit he bypassed on his way to bidding 3♠.

There is one more very important inference: responder must have a club control. Without a club control himself, responder would logically sign off in 4♠, regardless of the rest of his hand, as opener has denied a control. Two top club losers will doom any slam.

MORE ON INFERENTIAL CUEBIDS

The art of cuebidding can become quite complicated when one enters the world of inference.

Take a simple example.

WEST	EAST
1♥	2♣
2♦	2♥
2NT	

So far, we know *by definition* that opener holds poor trumps (no two of the top three honors). We also know *by virtue of a bypassed cuebid* that opener lacks the ability to cuebid 2♠, meaning that opener has no control in spades. This is the simplest kind of inference — a value is missing if it could have been shown and was not.

Change the auction slightly. Instead of 2NT, what if opener cuebids 3♣?

WEST	EAST
1♡	2♣
2◇	2♡
3♣	

Now, we know *by definition* that opener holds one of the top three honors in clubs. We also know *by virtue of a bypassed cuebid* that opener, again, lacks a spade control. Further, we know *by virtue of a bypassed cuebid* that opener holds two of the top three honors in hearts. The third inference is not radically different, but it illustrates the principle that bypassing a value-denying cuebid is an action that confirms holding those values.

Inference gets more interesting. Let's continue with the auction where opener bids 3♣, as shown. If responder now bids 3◇, we know *by definition* that responder holds a diamond card — one of the top three honors. However, we also know more than that. The purpose of cuebidding is to explore slam. Since opener lacks a spade control, if responder also lacked a spade control, he could, and would, simply sign off in 4♡ after the 3♣ cuebid. Further cuebidding would be pointless. Hence, when responder bids 3◇ in this auction, we know *by logical inference* that responder has a spade control.

Suppose that responder does bid 3◇. What if opener now cuebids 3♠? Things get interesting. We know *from prior bidding* that opener cannot have first- or second-round control of spades. Accordingly, 3♠ must show third-round spade control. We also know *from prior bidding* that opener has two top heart honors; therefore, when he bypasses 3♡ as a cuebid, we know that he lacks the ability to show something more in hearts, meaning that he lacks the third top heart honor.

The art of cuebidding requires that each partner recognize the correct inferences that can be drawn from each cuebid. Otherwise, incorrect inference builds on incorrect inference and entire cuebidding sequences crumble into absurdity.

Inferences Above the Cuebid

Inferential cuebidding can become rather complicated. Consider this auction:

WEST	EAST
1♠	2♣
2♡	2♠
3♣	3♠
4♣	

When responder cuebids 3♠, we know that he has the missing third spade honor, because opener's 3♣ cuebid, a bypass of 2NT, promised good trumps. Responder also denied a diamond control, because he bypassed 3◇, and similarly denied any top honor in hearts.

What about opener's 4♣ call? Since 3♣ showed one of the top three honors in clubs, 4♣ must show two top club honors. But we know more than that. Even though opener has not yet been able to cuebid diamonds, we know by logic that he has a diamond control — without one, he would simply sign off, since responder denied control of diamonds in the previous round of cuebids.

This is an example of an inference that is 'above' the present cuebid. We know, in many auctions, that if a control has already been denied by one partner (in a suit potentially biddable in the future by the other partner), then the other partner must hold a control in that suit. As a result, if he ever gets to that cuebid, and makes it, he will be showing extra control.

So, in our example, suppose opener cuebids 3NT instead of 4♣, and responder cuebids 4♣.

WEST	EAST
1♠	2♣
2♡	2♠
3♣	3♠
3NT	4♣
4◇	

We have just seen that 3NT by opener already implied a diamond control. So opener need not cuebid 4◇ just to show a diamond control. That would be redundant. If logic dictates that you must have a control in a specific suit (because you are still cuebidding in other suits), then it is not necessary to make a cuebid in that specific suit to show that control.

In this auction, what would 4◊ by opener show? Perhaps it clarifies that the control is first-round rather than second-round. Perhaps it shows both first- and second-round control. The limitations of the auction, logic, and the like dictate which meaning should be attributed. Generally, this bid will indicate first-round control, as opposed to second-round control.

Similar analysis can be done with respect to trump quality or contextually critical secondary fits. For example, if one player has first denied good trumps and then denied any top trump honor, any cuebid by partner must imply at least decent trumps. This may seem obvious, but the subtlety is often overlooked. Frequently, failure to cuebid a control that has already been implied gets mistaken as a denial of that control. Other times, a redundant cuebid will be under-evaluated as showing no better than simple control.

INFERENCES BELOW THE CUEBID

On the flip side of the coin of redundancy, a cuebid can imply a value in a suit that appears to have been bypassed. Consider this auction:

WEST	EAST
1♠	2◊
2♡	2♠
3♡	4◊

Spades were agreed when responder bid 2♠. Opener, by bidding 3♡, showed two top heart honors directly, implied good trumps (he bypassed 2NT), implied no diamond help (he bypassed 3◊) and implied no club control (he bypassed 3♣). What, then, is responder's 4◊ call?

Directly, we know that responder holds two of the top three honors in diamonds, because that is the definition of the call. As a direct inference, we also know that responder is not serious about slam, because he did not cuebid 3NT. However, we know more inferentially.

Responder would simply sign off in 4♠ if he also lacked a club control, right? Therefore, 4◊ must show a club control. This is an example of a bypass that nonetheless implies a control in a potentially cuebiddable suit (4♣) that is not actually bid.

Redefining Prior Cuebids

Let's continue to explore our example. As we have just determined, cuebidding 4◇ must imply a club control. So what would a cuebid of 4♣, instead, show?

WEST	EAST
1♠	2◇
2♡	2♠
3♡	4♣

Things get sticky here. After opener's 3♡ call, responder bypasses 3♠ to bid 4♣. Therefore, responder must lack the third spade honor. Responder must, however, have a club control to make any move. With a club control and no serious slam interest, but slam hope, three cuebids are available — 4♣, 4◇ and 4♡.

By definition alone, 4♣ would show a club control, 4◇ would show two of the top three diamond honors and 4♡ would show the missing heart card. By inference, 4◇ would also show a club control, as would 4♡.

Can hope remain if responder holds a club control but no heart card and no second diamond honor? Certainly, especially if opener has a void in diamonds and solid hearts. Therefore, technically, responder may need to cuebid 4♣ with second-round control, even if he has no ability to cuebid 4◇ or 4♡.

In such a situation, 4♣ merely shows a control.

Suppose, however, that 4♣ is bid and opener cuebids 4◇, followed by 4♡ by responder.

WEST	EAST
1♠	2◇
2♡	2♠
3♡	4♣
4◇	4♡

As this cuebid is real, showing a heart card, we reflect back on why responder did not simply cuebid 4♡. The simple answer, in this situation, is that 4♣ was intended to show first-round club control.

Thus, a new principle arises. When you are guaranteed to hold a control in a specific suit, you can bypass that cuebid to make another cuebid and still imply the necessary control. If you neglect to take that course, but later in the auction it is clear that you could have done so, you imply a greater than expected holding in the necessary suit. In a sense, the 4♡ cuebid in this example, by 'proving' an ability to cuebid 4♡ directly and imply the club control, redefines the prior 4♣ cuebid as showing first-round control as opposed to second-round control.

You might object at this point. "Maybe the 4♣ call inferentially denies the ability to cuebid 4♡ directly, so that a late 4♡ call merely shows the jack of hearts." That's a valid objection. It might be the case that such an inference arises.

Let's reason it out. The bid of 4♣, in the example auction, showed the necessary club control. Since that control could have been inferentially shown by cuebidding 4◊ or 4♡ instead, 4♣ implied an inability to make those cuebids. Later cuebids in diamonds or hearts, therefore, would show lesser values than those suggested by the immediate cuebid.

This auction gets particularly complicated. One could argue that the 4♣ cuebid, followed by a 4♡ cuebid, shows one of these various possibilities:

1. First-round club control, plus a heart top honor;
2. Club control (1st or 2nd), plus the heart jack;
3. Club control (1st or 2nd), plus a heart top honor;
4. First-round club control, plus the heart jack.

So which is it to be? Option 3 can be ruled out as redundant. Option 2 should not be our choice, because knowledge of the nature of the club control is almost always more important than possession of a jack. Personally, I rule out Option 4, simply because I find it too bizarre.

The agreement should therefore be Option 1, namely that the late heart cuebid redefines, or defines more precisely, the prior club cuebid as first-round control.

Double Inferences

It is possible for two necessary controls to be in play. Consider this sequence:

WEST	EAST
1♡	1♠
2♠	3♡
3♠	3NT
?	

In this auction, responder's 3♡ sounded like a game try. However, his 3NT call, a Serious 3NT, proved that his 3♡ call was really a cuebid, showing good trumps, a heart card, but no minor-suit controls. Thus, opener needs to have control in both minors. At least one of them must be first-round to justify any further slam exploration.

In this situation, a 4♣ cuebid by opener would directly show a club control and also imply a diamond control. Similarly, opener's 4◊ cuebid would show a diamond control and imply a club control. Thus, each cuebid promises control of both minors. When this occurs, you bid the better control. Thus, 4♣ would promise first-round club control and imply second-round diamond control. Bidding 4◊ instead would promise first-round diamond control and imply second-round club control. With first-round control in both suits, cuebid 4♣, the cheaper first-round control. A double bypass (4♡), if a cuebid (as it would be here, with spades agreed), also shows first-round control in both suits.

- 3 -

DEFINING THE JUMPS

Now that we have looked at the basics of cuebidding, it's time to refine our sequences by exploring the meanings attached to jumps. To some extent, jump cuebids are system-dependent: if your system has few or no sequences where trumps are agreed at the two-level in a game-forcing auction, then the opportunities for jump cuebids are severely limited. If you can make use of them, though, they are invaluable, simply because jumps are precisely defined bids. Non-jump cuebidding sequences derive extra meaning from the failure to jump. If we add jumps to our cuebidding structure, we add an important layer of refinement to non-jump sequences.

THE PICTURE JUMP CUEBID

The Picture Jump Cuebid into a long side suit is defined precisely. The person making this jump promises a very good holding in his side suit and good trumps, but no side first-round or second-round controls; neither an honor nor shortness. This will show 5422 pattern if the person has bid two suits or possibly 5332 or 6322 if the person has raised a known long suit.

Here's an example as opener. You open 1♠ and partner responds 2♣. You rebid 2♦ and partner sets trumps with 2♠. You may now Picture Jump Cuebid to 4♦ (your second suit) to show a hand with (i) good trumps (at least two of the top three honors in spades), (ii) a very good holding in your side suit (at least three of the top four honors in diamonds) and (iii) no side first-round or second-round control. Clearly you must be 5-2-4-2 pattern for this action, something like, at worst:

♠ K Q 4 3 2   ♡ 3 2   ◇ K Q J 2   ♣ 3 2

Consider a few different hands after the following auction:

WEST	EAST
1♠	2♣
2◇	2♠
?	

♠ K Q 4 3 2   ♡ 2   ◇ A K Q 3   ♣ 9 3 2

This hand is wrong for a Picture Jump to 4◇, because you have a heart control.

♠ A J 10 9 8   ♡ J 8   ◇ A K J 4   ♣ 9 4

Tempting, but the spade suit lacks two top honors.

♠ A Q 10 6 3   ♡ 8 5   ◇ A K 10 9   ♣ 6 3

This is also close, but the diamonds are too weak — by definition, you need three of the top four honors.

♠ A Q 8 5 3   ♡ J 9   ◇ A Q J 2   ♣ 8 5

A classic hand for a Picture Jump Cuebid.

Now for an example as responder. Partner opens 1♡ and you respond 2♣. After partner rebids 2◇, you set trumps with 2♡ and partner cuebids 2♠:

WEST	EAST
1♡	2♣
2◇	2♡
2♠	?

At this point, you can make a Picture Jump Cuebid of 4♣, showing essentially the same type of hand as opener would show for a Picture Jump Cuebid. The difference is that you may have only three-card support for the major in this auction, so your pattern is often 5332 or 6322, something like:

♠ 7 4 2   ♡ K Q 8   ◇ Q 10   ♣ A Q J 6 5

Suppose, instead, that you held

♠ K Q 2   ♡ 8 4   ◇ A Q J 8   ♣ Q J 10 9

and heard partner open 1♠. If you respond 2♣, you will clearly never be able to make a Picture Jump Cuebid. Thinking ahead, you might decide instead on a 2♦ response, calculated to let you to make a 4♦ Picture Jump Cuebid later. Such strategic thinking in the early bidding will help you set up some nice calls.

AFTER A PICTURE JUMP

If you poll popular opinion, the usual view is that the purpose of a call like the Picture Jump Cuebid is to give absolute information to partner, describing your hand with one bid and enabling partner to assume captaincy. The thought has been that partner will know so much about your hand that he should simply be able to place the contract.

Although it is true that such a descriptive bid should transfer captaincy of the auction to partner, it is not so certain that partner will have enough information to place the final contract. Partner may, for instance, be short in your great suit. Partner may very well have an equally sound suit of his own needing some contribution from you, perhaps in the form of lesser honors. Partner may be uncertain as to the situation in the fourth suit, perhaps because he fears the lead coming through his K-6-2; partner may even have lingering doubts about the trump suit.

When partner makes a Picture Jump Cuebid, the following four domains should form the basis of any further inquiries during the rest of the bidding:

1. **YOUR** suit. How good is the Picture Jump side suit? How many Quick Tricks will it provide? In other words, which honor, if any, is missing?

2. **MY** suit. Do you have any help for my side suit (if any was shown)? Do you perhaps have the jack, the queen, or both?

3. **THEIR** suit. I might have the K-x-(x) and fear this lead. You cannot have the ace (your Picture Jump denied side-suit controls). Do you, by any chance, have the queen?

4. **OUR** suit. You have at least two top honors in our suit, but I may have nothing. Or, perhaps, I fear a 4-1 split and losing a trump trick to the jack in a grand slam. How many of the top four honors do you hold in our suit? Which ones? Do you have any extra length?

You will easily see that none of these potential questions can be answered well with, for example, Roman Keycard Blackwood. Specialized asking bids might do the trick. For this reason, I propose the use of four asking bids, one for each potential question partner might want to ask. These four asking bids are the Your Suit asking bid, the My Suit asking bid, the Their Suit asking bid, and the Our Suit asking bid.

Employing the 'useful space' principle, I also suggest that these asking bids be ordered as to priority, in the same order as set forth above. It seems to me that the four potential questions are fairly ordered in terms of likely importance in real life. A useful mnemonic device I use is 'Yummy Toes' ('yu' for 'Your suit', 'mmy' for 'My suit', 't' for 'Their suit', and 'oes' for 'Our suit'). It may sound a touch weird, but it's going to be hard to forget that you and partner use Yummy Toes Asking Bids, right?

Anyway, the idea behind this structure is that the first relay available asks the first question, the second asks the second, and so forth, skipping steps where necessary (the game bid, for example). The next round of bidding starts another relay, in priority order again, with the asked question skipped. Calls of 4NT and 5NT are used as asking bids also.

Without examples to explain what I mean, this initial description will make no sense to you, I expect. Let's take a simple auction as the starting point. Partner opens 1♠ and you respond 2♣. Partner rebids 2◇ and you set trumps with 2♠, at which point partner makes a Picture Jump Cuebid of 4◇.

WEST	EAST
1♠	2♣
2◇	2♠
4◇	?

Of course, you might lose interest rapidly and sign off in 4♠. Suppose, however, that you do have interest in slam, but still have lingering questions.

First, you should remember the mnemonic device 'yummy toes'. Then you can ask your questions with the following four steps (skipping the trump suit, of course):

First Step	4♡	First Question	'How good is YOUR suit?'
Trump Suit	4♠	Natural, signoff	
Second Step	4NT	Second Question	'How good is your holding in MY suit?
Third Step	5♣	Third Question	'How good is your holding in THEIR suit?'
Fourth Step	5◊	Fourth Question	'How good is your trump holding, OUR suit?'

Suppose your most pressing concern is your own suit, clubs. After 4◊, you might very well make the My Suit asking bid of 4NT, the second step in the priority list. Suppose partner's answer (the answers will be explained shortly) is 5◊, confirming a slam and making even a grand slam possible. Now, you may have decided that the answer to another of the three possible remaining questions is critical to the grand slam. Removing the second question, already answered, and conserving useful space, you end up with the following options:

First Step	5♡	First Question	'How good is YOUR suit?'
Trump Suit	5♠	Natural, signoff	
Second Step	5NT	Third Question	'How good is your holding in THEIR suit?'
Third Step	6♣	Fourth Question	'How good is your TRUMP holding?'

This process of picking relevant questions can continue according to the Yummy Toes order until all questions are answered. You can change the precise order of questions by skipping to a desired first question and then perhaps returning to a skipped question later. This is done because the default order of priority may not establish the actual priority for a given deal. Some answers might be relevant to a small slam decision, perhaps with one of those answers opening up unexpected chances for a grand slam, making a skipped question suddenly relevant again.

What, then, are the answers to the four base questions? These are each relatively simple and logical.

The Your Suit Answers

The Your Suit asking bid is designed to find out the strength of your suit. Not only will partner find out how many tricks he can count on there, but also how quickly they can be developed. In a simple example, partner might have no use for your suit except as quick pitches. A suit like K-Q-J-10-9 produces no quick pitches to get rid of losers in a side suit like A-x-x, assuming that the opponents lead the side suit. However, A-K-Q-3-2 fits the bill. You also have to consider that a suit like A-Q-J-10-9 is less likely to produce four tricks without a loser than a suit like A-K-Q-10-5.

This, then, is the answer structure:

Step One	No Quick Tricks	Missing the Ace	K-Q-J-x-(x)
Step Two	One Quick Trick	Missing the King	A-Q-J-x-(x)
Step Three	Two Quick Tricks	Missing the Queen	A-K-J-x-(x)
Step Four	Three Quick Tricks	Missing the Jack	A-K-Q-x-(x)
Step Five	Four Quick Tricks	Solid	A-K-Q-J-(x)

Notice that the order of responses is from weakest to strongest, which will be true of all our asking bids. This method not only keeps you lower when you may want to get out before the six-level, but it also, as a general rule, helps you to remember the response structure.

The My Suit Answers

With the My Suit asking bid, partner is inquiring about any contributions you might have that will solidify his suit. Perhaps he has a singleton in your suit but a semi-solid suit of his own. You are not the only person entitled to have a great side suit, you know! The limitations of the Picture Jump Cuebid place tight restraints on your potential support for partner's suit: since you deny side-suit controls, you cannot provide the ace or king. Thus, the step responses are rather simple:

Step One	I have nothing for you.
Step Two	I have the jack.
Step Three	I have the queen.
Step Four	I have both the queen and the jack.

Again, the responses go from weakest to strongest.

The Their Suit Answers

When partner uses a Their Suit ask, he is asking you to help him with a specific concern. Remember, you have already denied a control in this suit, so that is not the issue. The usual reason for this question is concern about a lead of the fourth suit through dummy and the potential loss of two quick tricks. For this reason, we expect the asker to be interested in a small slam only and to have K-x-(x) in the side suit. As you cannot have the ace to help him, the only thing that can be of interest is whether or not you have the missing queen. As a result, the answers to this question are simple:

Step One	Bad News — I do not have the queen.
Step Two	Good News — I have the queen.

The Our Suit Answers

This time, partner is asking for more information about your trump holding, and there are two likely reasons for this. First, partner may himself have a horrible trump holding. Trash like 6-4-2 opposite K-Q-7-5-3 is a risky trump suit for a slam, but 10-9-8 opposite K-Q-J-7-6 works fine, usually. Second, partner may be thinking about bidding a slam that will rely on a successful finesse, at best a 50-50 venture; he needs trumps to be solid to keep the odds at 50-50. Third, partner may be contemplating a grand slam on an eight-card fit and be unwilling to risk a J-x-x-x stack in trumps.

The answers to the Our Suit asking bid should, therefore, advise partner of our trump honors (remember: the Picture Jump already promised at least two of the top three). He needs to know whether we can reduce the chances of having two trump losers or if we can solidify the suit with a third or fourth honor in trumps. The answers are as follows:

First Step	Two top honors only
Second Step	Two top honors, plus the jack
Third Step	All three top honors
Fourth Step	A-K-Q-J

WRAP-AROUND ANSWERING

As with any asking bid structure, the Yummy Toes asking bids can be further economized using a technique known as 'zoom' or 'wrap-around'. (Consumer advisory: this is going to get complicated, but once you get the hang of it, I think you'll like it.) Suppose your answer to the current asking bid is the best possible answer — the last step, whatever that is. Further suppose that your answer leaves only one bid, or none at all, between your call and the next level of our agreed suit. For example, consider the situation where hearts are trumps, the current asking bid was a Your Suit asking bid, and your answer was 5♣, which happened to show that your suit was solid (A-K-Q-J-x). Partner has only one asking bid left, namely 5◇. Surely, though, your great response will enable him to bid a slam, unless, perhaps, he needs one other specific question answered, namely whatever would be asked by bidding 5◇. You can save him space and just answer that question right now.

Let's look at an example of how this would work. After you open 1♠, partner responds 2♣. You rebid 2◇ and partner sets trumps with 2♠. You can now make a Picture Jump Cuebid of 4◇. If partner now makes a Your Suit asking bid (4♡), your best possible answer is 5♡, showing a solid suit. That answer must be very encouraging, but it leaves partner with no possible cuebid below 5♠. The auction so far:

WEST	EAST
1♠	2♣
2◇	2♠
4◇¹	4♡²
5♡³	?

1. Picture Jump Cuebid.
2. Your Suit (diamonds) asking bid.
3. Solid diamonds.

Instead of this simple approach, let's look at a scheme of wrap-around answering. If your answer to the first asking bid shows the best possible answer, and if that answer leaves only one possible cuebid below the next level of commitment (or no bid, if the answer is at or one below the trump suit), then you simply answer the next question at the same time. After 4♡ in the example (Your Suit asking bid), an answer of 5♡ would normally just show a solid suit, the best possible holding. If we are using the space-saving technique, 5♡ would show the best possible answer (a solid suit) with a step-one response to the next asking bid in priority order. Here, that is a My Suit asking bid, so the first step (5♡) would mean no help in partner's suit, clubs. Bidding 5♠ instead would still show that your diamond suit is solid, but would also show the jack in support of partner's suit. The last two possibilities are 5NT and 6♣. 5NT would show that your diamond suit is solid and that you have the queen of clubs. 6♣ would show solid diamonds with the Q-J of clubs.

Thus, in response to a 4♡ Your Suit asking bid (in our example), the possible answers would be as follows:

		Your Suit Answers	**My Suit Answers**
4♠	=	Missing the Ace (K-Q-J-x)	—
4NT	=	Missing the King (A-Q-J-x)	—
5♣	=	Missing the Queen (A-K-J-x)	—
5♢	=	Missing the Jack (A-K-Q-x)	—
5♡	=	Solid (A-K-Q-J), with	no help in clubs
5♠	=	Solid (A-K-Q-J), with	J-x in clubs
5NT	=	Solid (A-K-Q-J), with	Q-x in clubs
6♣	=	Solid (A-K-Q-J), with	Q-J in clubs

A 6♣ answer here is the best possible answer to the second question. In other words, you have great news, twice! So if you like, the secondary question-answer could wrap also, to complete a Their Suit asking bid, such that:

6♣	=	Solid diamonds	Q-J in clubs	No queen of hearts
6♢	=	Solid diamonds	Q-J in clubs	Queen of hearts

Why stop? Madness is fun! The 6♢ answer would further wrap, on to an Our Suit asking bid (never bypassing six of our major unless the original asking bid was a grand slam try), as follows:

6♢	=	Solid, Q-J of clubs, queen of hearts, two top spades
6♡	=	Solid, Q-J of clubs, queen of hearts, two plus the jack
6♠	=	Solid, Q-J of clubs, queen of hearts, A-K-Q+ of spades

This idea can be applied at any stage of any asking bid auction. Back up a tad and let's look at what would happen if the initial first-round 'wrap' was

5NT, showing a solid suit, but only Q-x in clubs. This club holding is not the 'best possible answer', as it denies possessing the club jack.

Now partner might bid 6♣ after your 5NT answer, which would be a Their Suit asking bid (the next priority asking bid, since we've already answered Your Suit and My Suit). If you lacked the side queen, you'd bid 6◇. With the side queen, you would normally bid 6♡, but that would deprive partner of the Our Suit asking bid. Instead, you would further compact this second round of asking bids, so that 6◇ would show no side queen, 6♡ would show the side queen (best possible answer) with only two top spades (Our Suit asking bid response #1), 6♠ would show the side queen plus the jack of trumps, and 6NT would show the side queen with all three top spade honors (because 6♣ was clearly in pursuit of a grand slam). A response of 7♣ would show the side queen and four solid spades. Hence, our side would be committed to the seven-level, even after all maximum responses, only if everything that could be useful was held. Granted, opener can't really have all these cards in this auction, else the opening bid would have been 2♣ not 1♠. But you must see the beauty of this possibility.

Let's look more closely at what I have just put forward with a real-world example. You are dealt:

♠ K Q 4 3 2   ♡ 3 2   ◇ A K Q J   ♣ 3 2

You open 1♠, partner bids 2♣, you rebid 2◇ and partner sets trumps with 2♠. After a Picture Jump to 4◇, partner bids 4♡, a Your Suit asking bid.

YOU	PARTNER
1♠	2♣
2◇	2♠
4◇	4♡
?	

Holding solid diamonds, your answer would normally be a simple 5♡, the fifth step. Since we 'wrap around' the final step in this situation, you must first assess the My Suit assistance — clubs. Lacking any help, your fifth-step answer of 5♡ is maintained, showing solid diamonds (My Suit) without help in clubs (Your Suit).

Change the hand slightly to

$$\spadesuit K Q 4 3 2 \quad \heartsuit 3 2 \quad \diamondsuit A K Q J \quad \clubsuit J 2$$

and instead of answering 5♡, showing no help in clubs, your answer to the My Suit ask requires an additional step. Hence, a call of 5♠, the sixth step, shows a step-five response to the Your Suit ask (solid), with a second-step wrap-around in clubs (the jack). Similarly, the response of 5NT, the seventh step, would show:

$$\spadesuit K Q 4 3 2 \quad \heartsuit 3 2 \quad \diamondsuit A K Q J \quad \clubsuit Q 2$$

Suppose you have instead:

$$\spadesuit K Q 4 3 2 \quad \heartsuit 3 2 \quad \diamondsuit A K Q J \quad \clubsuit Q J$$

Again, the diamond holding is the best possible, starting your next question with 5♡ and higher. As a holding of queen-jack in clubs is the fourth step up, the wrap-around response would be 6♣. Hence, in response to partner's 4♡ asking bid, a leap to 6♣ shows your holdings in diamonds and clubs through wrap-around answering.

As you already guessed, it gets better. The 6♣ response leaves room between 6♣ and 6♠, the agreed trump fit. The next question by priority is Their Suit. Thus, 6♣ actually shows

$$\spadesuit K Q 4 3 2 \quad \heartsuit 3 2 \quad \diamondsuit A K Q J \quad \clubsuit Q J$$

with no help in Their Suit, whereas 6♢ shows

$$\spadesuit K Q 4 3 2 \quad \heartsuit Q 2 \quad \diamondsuit A K Q J \quad \clubsuit Q J$$

— the hand with the ♡Q. Thus, wrapping around the answers enables you to gain increasingly precise information, refining hand definition when the answers are the best possible.

Here's an example of the Picture Jump Cuebid and the follow-up auction in practice:

WEST	EAST
♠ A Q J 3 2	♠ K 8 5
♡ 7 3	♡ A 5 4
◇ A K Q 8	◇ 9 6 3
♣ J 5	♣ A K Q 2

WEST	EAST
1♠	2♣
2◇	2♠
?	

West is stronger than minimum for the bid, but a 4◇ Picture Jump Cuebid seems ideal. By definition, it is appropriate.

Responder can now picture strong slam possibilities. Since West is known to have 5-2-4-2 pattern, it's likely that there are at most two losers (one diamond and one heart), so it is worth exploring for slam. The first priority is the diamond strength, so East wields the 'Your Suit' asking bid, 4♡.

West has all three top honors in diamonds, missing the jack. This being the fourth step, his answer would be 5◇. This leaves East with only one asking bid below 5♠, the 'My Suit' asking bid (first of the remaining possibilities, in priority). However, 5◇ was not the best possible answer to the asking bid, so no wrap-around answering is available. East, however, can 'see' that twelve tricks will probably be easy to find, so it seems reasonable to ask the next question. Responder bids 5♡, asking about 'My Suit', clubs.

West is safe to continue past 5♠, as East must have made allowances for a 5NT response (J-x). West bids 5NT, showing J-x of clubs. Again, as this is not the 'best possible answer', no wrap-around answering is done.

This is great news for East. He can now count four tricks in clubs, three in diamonds, one in hearts and probably five in spades, for thirteen tricks. If the contest is IMP scoring or if the field is conservative, he might opt to be conservative and check on protection against a 4-1 spade split. The 'Our Suit' asking bid is the second of the remaining asking bids, so East bids 6◇.

Opener does not have all three top honors, but he does have the jack. This is the second step answer, so he bids 6♠. This solidifies trumps for responder, so he can confidently bid 7♠ or even 7NT. How proud we are! Who else could have found two of the three key jacks and known that the other jack (of diamonds) was missing?

The complete auction:

WEST	EAST
1♠	2♣
2◊	2♠
4◊[1]	4♡[2]
5◊[3]	5♡[4]
5NT[5]	6◊[6]
6♠[7]	7♠/7NT

1. Picture Jump Cuebid.
2. Your Suit (diamonds) asking bid.
3. A-K-Q, no jack.
4. My Suit (clubs) asking bid.
5. J-x of clubs.
6. Our Suit asking bid.
7. Only two top spade honors, but with the jack.

THE DELAYED PICTURE JUMP CUEBID

Now, let's move on to look at a Picture Jump Cuebid that is made after a cuebid or two. We may be able to infer more about a hand that makes such a Picture Jump Cuebid than if it had been made as the first cuebid.

You wouldn't make a Picture Jump Cuebid just for the fun of it. Rather, you would do so when slam is contextually possible. Thus a Picture Jump Cuebid cannot logically deny control of a suit in which partner also denied control. With

♠ K Q 4 3 2   ♡ 3 2   ◊ K Q J 2   ♣ 3 2

for example, you have a minimum holding for a Picture Jump Cuebid. However, if partner has already denied first- or second-round control of clubs, there would be no point in making a Picture Jump Cuebid, as slam has been ruled out. If you make one anyway, then you must have a club control. Change the hand slightly to include the club king and this would be the new 'minimum' after partner has denied a club control.

Let's look at the specific inferences that can be drawn from a delayed Picture Jump Cuebid.

JUMPER HOLDS A PREVIOUSLY DENIED SIDE CONTROL

Suppose the auction starts like this:

WEST	EAST
1♡	2♣
2◇	2♡
?	

Now suppose opener cuebids 2NT, showing poor trumps and denying a spade control (he did not cuebid 2♠). Normally, a Picture Jump Cuebid of 4♣ by responder would show two top heart honors, three of the top four honors in clubs but no controls in spades or diamonds.

WEST	EAST
1♡	2♣
2◇	2♡
2NT	4♣

This makes little sense, however, after opener has denied a spade control. East would hardly make a slam try with no spade control himself. So a late Picture Jump Cuebid inferentially promises a second-round control in a suit in which partner has denied control. (With first-round control, normal cuebidding should continue, without using a Picture Jump.) This restriction to second-round control is purely a matter of definition, but it helps to facilitate subsequent bidding. If the side control could be the ace or the king or a void or a singleton or a singleton ace or a singleton king or K-Q or A-Q or A-K, etc., then the asking bid sequences to distinguish among these possibilities would be ridiculously complex.

For reasons that will be apparent shortly (the availability of a Picture Splinter to show a singleton), this second-round control is in fact always the king. When a Picture Jump Cuebid inferentially shows second-round control in a side suit, then the asking bid for this inferential control is, obviously, adjusted. In the example auction, 4♣ promises the spade king: second-round spade control. Logically, then, the responses to a Their Suit asking bid should be changed to reflect the depth of control, i.e. whether the queen is also held. If a Their Suit asking bid is made after a Picture Jump has implied a control in 'their suit', the responses are modified as follows:

> First Step   Tepid Second-Round Control (K-x)
> Second Step   Sound Second-Round Control (K-Q)

JUMPER HAS A LESSER TRUMP CONTRIBUTION

Suppose the auction starts like this:

WEST	EAST
1♠	2◇
2♡	2♠
?	

If opener now cuebids 3♣, he shows a club control and also promises good trumps (two of the top three honors), because he did not cuebid 2NT (poor trumps). Therefore, in this sequence, responder cannot also have two top spade honors. As a result, it makes sense that a 4◇ Picture Jump should be available to responder if he holds the remaining top honor, confirming solid top trumps for the partnership.

WEST	EAST
1♠	2◇
2♡	2♠
3♣	4◇

Logically, this would adjust the responses to the Our Suit asking bid, as follows:

> First Step   I do not have the jack
> Second Step   I also have the jack

JUMPER HAS AN EXTRA SIDE-SUIT CONTROL

This principle of changed definitions for Picture Jumps can be extended even further. Suppose the auction starts like this:

WEST	EAST
1♠	2♣
2♡	2♠
?	

Now opener cuebids 3♣ (good trumps plus a club honor) and responder cuebids 3♢ (diamond control). What does it imply if opener now makes a delayed Picture Jump Cuebid to 4♡?

WEST	EAST
1♠	2♣
2♡	2♠
3♣	3♢
4♡	

If opener held no club control and no diamond control, he would have made this Picture Jump Cuebid earlier. Thus, something must be different. Obviously, we know from the prior 3♣ cuebid that a first- or second-round club control was the difference, and this information has to be included in our asking bid responses. Thus, if responder makes a 'My Suit' asking bid, the responses are as follows:

First Step	I just have the control I showed, the ace or king
Second Step	I have a top honor, plus the queen
Third Step	I have two top honors
Fourth Step	I have two top honors, plus the queen

These responses are modified because we know two things. First, opener must have the ace, king or queen of clubs for his 3♣ call. Second, with only the queen, he could have made a Picture Jump of 4♡ over 2♠. Therefore, opener must have the ace or king of clubs, at a minimum.

If the side-suit control previously cuebid was 'Their Suit', the answers are different. Change the auction:

WEST	EAST
1♠	2♦
2♡	2♠
3♣	3♦
4♡	

The club cuebid was not in support of responder's suit and could, therefore, be shortness. A singleton, however, would have been handled with a Picture Splinter (coming up soon). Thus, the Their Suit responses would be as follows:

First Step	Second-round control (the king)
Second Step	First-round control (the ace)
Third Step	Double control (A-K or a void)

JUMPER IS KNOWN TO HAVE LESSER TRUMPS

If the Jump Cuebid is made by a partner who has previously shown poor trumps by cuebidding 2NT, then the responses to the 'Our Suit' asking bid are also changed, as follows:

First Step	One of the top three honors
Second Step	One of the top three honors, plus the jack

This might occur, for example, after the following auction:

WEST	EAST
1♠	2♣
2♦	2♠
2NT	3♣
4♦	

Opener must have no club control, no heart control, only one top spade and great diamonds. Simple, right?

Fortunately, this principle of implied modifications to the requirements for a delayed Picture Jump Cuebid can be played out in only a limited number of sequences. The largest number of cuebids possible before a Delayed Picture Jump Cuebid is illustrated by this auction:

WEST	EAST
1♠	2♣
2♡	2♠
2NT	3♣
3◇	4♡

You should notice that, in this auction, the Delayed Picture Jump is made by the person who made only one prior cuebid. Hence, only one inference is possible to modify the meaning: a club control.

How about this one?

WEST	EAST
1♠	2♣
2♡	2♠
3♣	3◇
4♡	

In this auction, the 3♣ cuebid permits a double inference that West has good trumps and a club card. However, the bypass of 2NT merely confirms good trumps, as defined by the normal Picture Jump Cuebid.

It seems, therefore, that the four inferential changes to normal Picture Jump Cuebids and the five resulting modifications of the Yummy Toes Asking Bids after these modified Picture Jump Cuebids are the only changes possible, making it a less daunting task to memorize the amended Yummy Toes situations.

THE PICTURE SPLINTER

The Picture Splinter is very similar to the Picture Jump Cuebid. It is a jump during a cuebidding sequence (or a jump that initiates a cuebidding sequence) into any unbid suit or into a suit only bid by partner. It shows the exact same holdings as the Picture Jump Cuebid, except that this time it shows a singleton in the suit into which you jump. For example, suppose you open 1♠, partner responds 2♣, you rebid 2♡ and partner sets trumps by bidding 2♠. If you now make a Picture Splinter to 4◇, you should have something like:

♠ A Q 6 5 3　♡ A Q J 7　◇ 7　♣ 5 4 3

As before, you have two of the top three spade honors, three of the top four honors in your own side suit (hearts) and no club control. This time, in addition, you have a singleton in diamonds. If you made a Picture Splinter to 4♣ instead, you would have the same type of hand, with clubs and diamonds reversed.

WEST	EAST
1♠	2♣
2♡	2♠
4♣/4◇	

The Picture Splinter concept (i.e. needing specific honor holdings in trumps and your own second suit before being able to make a splinter bid) will be foreign to most readers, as people love to use splinter bids. You might ask why strict adherence to the parameters of a Picture Jump Cuebid is required when making a splinter bid. Following this rule, of course, is no more 'required' than is using Italian cuebidding generally. However, precisely defining a splinter bid as a 'Picture Splinter' adds clarity to that call, with alternative auctions using regular cuebids, or even delayed jumps, being used on the 'imperfect' hands.

Consider the following hands and think about which of them opener could hold after the following auction:

WEST	EAST
1♠	2♣
2♡	2♠
4◇	

♠ A Q 6 5 3　♡ A Q 10 9　◇ 7　♣ 5 4 3

This is wrong for a Picture Splinter, because partner will be relying on better hearts from you (three of the top four honors).

♠ A J 10 7 6　♡ A Q J 10　◇ 7　♣ 5 4 3

This is also wrong, because partner will expect you to have the A-K of spades if he holds Q-3-2.

$\spadesuit$ A Q 5 3 2 $\heartsuit$ A Q J 8 $\diamondsuit$ 7 $\clubsuit$ K 10 8

Here the Picture Splinter would be wrong, as partner will expect your clubs to be weak, and he has no way to ask for clarification of that issue.

$\spadesuit$ K Q 8 6 3 $\heartsuit$ K Q J 4 $\diamondsuit$ 7 $\clubsuit$ 9 8 5

This is a terrible opening hand, at best a dead minimum. A Picture Splinter will show where your values are, very precisely.

Just as with Picture Jump Cuebids, a Picture Jump Splinter may be a delayed act and partner can infer what caused the delay. For example, after this auction,

WEST	EAST
1$\spadesuit$	2$\clubsuit$
2$\diamondsuit$	2$\spadesuit$
?	

suppose opener cuebids 3$\clubsuit$ (good trumps, plus a club honor) and responder cuebids 3$\diamondsuit$ (a diamond honor). What if opener now makes a Delayed Picture Splinter of 4$\heartsuit$?

WEST	EAST
1$\spadesuit$	2$\clubsuit$
2$\diamondsuit$	2$\spadesuit$
3$\clubsuit$	3$\diamondsuit$
4$\heartsuit$	

We know that he must have a flaw for the original 4$\heartsuit$ option. His flaw cannot be trumps, as his 3$\clubsuit$ cuebid promised good trumps. The delayed action flaw would be the most logical. We know opener to have a top club honor. If that top honor were the queen, he would have made an earlier Picture Jump Splinter. Hence, we know that the top club honor is the ace or the king.

The Yummy Toes asking bids are still used, including the My Suit asking bid, even if you splinter into partner's suit. Partner may want to know if you have a singleton honor in his suit. You should not make a Picture Splinter with the singleton ace or singleton king, but you may still have the singleton queen or singleton jack. Obviously, you cannot have the singleton Q-J, so there are only three steps. The 'best possible' response is now the singleton queen.

You should note that with a hand that includes a singleton, you may have a fifth card in the secondary suit, or a sixth card in the primary suit, either of which is possible if the fourth suit is only a doubleton. The card of extra length, if you have it, may be shown as a false jack if you feel like being aggressive. Partner, if he holds the jack, will easily understand what feature you are trying to show.

You should also note that a Picture Splinter should not be made with two singletons or with a void.

Here's an example of the Picture Splinter in action:

WEST	EAST
♠ A K 10 8 7	♠ Q 6 3
♡ 7 6 5	♡ K 2
◇ K Q J 8	◇ A 7
♣ 2	♣ A K 6 5 4 3

Opener starts, of course, by opening 1♠. Responder creates a game-force with 2♣ and opener shows his diamond suit by rebidding 2◇. Responder sets trumps with a call of 2♠.

WEST	EAST
1♠	2♣
2◇	2♠
?	

Opener has a six-loser hand with a singleton club and concentrated values in spades and diamonds. This meets the definition of a Picture Splinter — good trumps (at least two top honors), great diamonds (three of the top four honors) and lack of a heart control. Accordingly, opener jumps to 4♣.

Responder counts tricks. With spades cooperating (3-2 split), he expects five spades, four diamonds and eventually at least three established clubs, for twelve tricks — a small slam. However, he expects a certain loser in the form of the heart ace on the expected heart lead. The sole question responder has is whether this small slam is greater than or worse than 50%. If the heart suit can be held to one loser, the slam is a good bet to make whenever spades split 3-2, making it a reasonable shot. If, however, the heart ace is poorly placed, two quick heart losers are possible. If opener doesn't hold the heart queen, the heart situation is 50-50 to produce a second loser. Thus the slam would fail whenever the hearts do not cooperate (50% of the time), plus whenever spades or even clubs break poorly, making the contract odds-against. You can see, therefore, that the advisability of bidding the small slam turns on whether opener has the heart queen.

Accordingly, responder uses the Their Suit asking bid, the third step in Yummy Toes (Yours, Mine, Theirs, Ours) and bids 4NT, asking about the heart suit. On this hand, opener is not looking at the heart queen and he bids 5♣. This disappointing answer reduces the slam to less than 50-50, causing responder, who sees a potential twelve offensive tricks, to resign himself wisely to a 5♠ signoff.

On this deal, the partnership has a combined 29 HCP, plus a singleton, along with a good eight-card trump fit. However, slam is deemed against the odds, at a relatively low level. The complete auction:

WEST	EAST
1♠	2♣
2◊	2♠
4♣[1]	4NT[2]
5♣[3]	5♠
pass	

1. Picture Splinter.
2. Their Suit (hearts) asking bid (third step).
3. No heart queen.

Had opener held a slightly different hand,

♠ A K 10 8 7   ♡ Q 7 6   ◊ K Q J 8   ♣ 2

his response to the Their Suit ask would have been 5◊, and the small slam would be bid and likely made.

Here is another example of the Picture Splinter in use, this time with a more exciting finish (if you prefer finding good slams to avoiding bad ones):

WEST	EAST
♠ A K 10 4 2	♠ Q J 9
♡ 6 2	♡ K Q 8 4
◊ A Q J 5 4	◊ 10
♣ Q	♣ A K J 8 2

Opener starts with 1♠ and responder creates a game-force with 2♣. Opener now shows his second suit with 2◇ and responder sets trumps with a call of 2♠.

WEST	EAST
1♠	2♣
2◇	2♠
4♣	?

Opener has a perfect Picture Splinter of 4♣. Change his club to the singleton king and his club holding would be too strong for a Picture Splinter. A singleton queen is acceptable, however.

Responder now has an interesting problem. He likes his hand generally for slam, and yet this Picture Splinter call just exposed a certain heart loser and singletons opposite values. Fortunately, trumps at least are solid.

Responder realizes that his singleton does not help opener's suit, but that opener might have help in clubs. Accordingly, a My Suit asking bid seems advisable. That being the second Yummy Toes step, responder bids 4♡. Responder is safe asking this question, because the possible answers are 4♠ (no help) and 5♣ (the queen). The auction will not go past game unless the answer justifies bypassing game.

Opener is pleased by this asking bid, because he does in fact have the club queen, his 'best possible' response. A response of 4♠ would deny a singleton club honor and 4NT would show the singleton jack. Holding the singleton queen, opener bids 5♣. Since 5♣ allows room for two asking bids below 5♠ (5◇ as a 'Your Suit' asking bid and 5♡ as a 'Their Suit' asking bid), opener does not 'wrap around' to the next answer. Thus, 5♣ says nothing else than that he has the singleton queen of clubs.

Responder can now count five spades, four clubs and at least one heart, for ten tricks. An eleventh and twelfth seem likely, either from the hearts being placed well or the clubs splitting 4-3 or diamonds coming through. Thus, a Your Suit asking bid to clarify the diamond trick count and to ensure that two aces are not missing is in order. That asking bid is 5◇, the first step.

Opener has the diamond ace, but he is missing the king. He gives the second step answer: 5♠. This makes slam a strong bet and responder can confidently try for twelve tricks, bidding 6♠. The auction:

WEST	EAST
1♠	2♣
2♦	2♠
4♣[1]	4♡[2]
5♣[3]	5♦[4]
5♠[5]	6♠

1. Picture Splinter.
2. My Suit (clubs) asking bid.
3. Singleton queen of clubs.
4. Your Suit (diamonds) asking bid.
5. The ace without the king.

As a final comment on the Picture Splinter, I will add that I have a personal preference for using the Picture Splinter as often as possible, including with three-level jumps by opener in game-forcing auctions. Thus, in the recommended approach, we abandon any natural meaning for the jump shift after a game force has been established, opting instead to maximize the use of the Picture Splinter. Fortunately, this is an unusual treatment only in a limited number of auctions, the most common of which involve opening 1♠ and then jumping to 3♡ after a game-forcing minor response, or opening a major and then jumping to 3♦ after a 2♣ game-forcing response. These are the four auctions:

WEST	EAST		WEST	EAST
1♠	2♣		1♠	2♦
3♡			3♡	

WEST	EAST		WEST	EAST
1♠	2♣		1♡	2♣
3♦			3♦	

In these auctions, a jump shift according to your current agreements might show extra length and/or strength. With suitable hands, I recommend that you simply rebid the new suit without a jump and hope to show the extra strength later. For my part, I like to play that these jump shifts agree the last-bid suit from partner and are Picture Splinter bids.

Of course, if you think this suggestion is an unusual treatment for good reason, then please keep that in mind when reviewing future example hands.

THE PICTURE JUMP TO 3NT

Playing with a very good friend of mine, I once jumped to 3NT in an unusual auction, intending to show that my initial four-card major raise was really bid on three-card support. Partner took this as Serious, which caused me great amusement: the 'Leaping Serious 3NT', apparently showing *really* serious interest in a slam. Since that day, I have seen no discussion of what a leap to 3NT should actually show in a cuebidding sequence.

I propose a rather simple idea. The Picture Jump to 3NT should show good trumps (two or more top honors), two of the top three honors and a total of three cards in partner's suit and no control in my own second suit. Inferentially, this will show a singleton in the fourth suit, if it is opener who makes the bid. Note that a Picture Jump to 3NT can be made only after a major has already been agreed on, meaning that a jump to 3NT is never used to set trumps.

Consider this example:

WEST	EAST
1♠	2♣
2♡	2♠
?	

Suppose that you, as opener, have a hand like:

♠ A Q 6 5 3   ♡ Q 9 8 7   ◇ 5   ♣ K Q 4

With this, you have a great Picture Jump to 3NT.

You will probably realize quickly that this jump will require some modification to the subsequent Yummy Toes asking bids. The Your Suit asking bid is still the first step, but you would answer it like a Their Suit asking bid, informing partner whether or not you have the queen (to protect his possible K-9 from a lead). After all, you don't have the ace or king and you might have J-8-6-5 or worse.

The My Suit asking bid is still the second step, but your answers are like a Your Suit asking bid, namely informing partner which top honor is missing. The first step shows a missing ace (K-Q-x), the second the missing king (A-Q-x) and the third step the missing queen (A-K-x). For conservative partnerships, where the initial 2/1 response promises a decent suit, the My Suit asking bid might be dropped as unnecessary (resulting in 'Yu Toes' asking bids), but I need this asking bid to protect partners (and myself) who sometimes bid trashy four-card suits to deflect that lead.

The Their Suit asking bid is completely unnecessary and should be dropped, yielding 'Yummy O' for the wild folks and 'Y.O.' for the succinct.

The Our Suit asking bid remains identical.

An example of the Picture Jump to 3NT in use:

WEST	EAST
♠ K Q 9 8 5	♠ A 6 4
♡ Q 10 5 4	♡ K
◇ K Q 2	◇ A 9 5 4 3
♣ 10	♣ A 8 5 4

Opener starts 1♠, hears 2◇, rebids 2♡ and hears 2♠, setting trumps. His hearts are lousy, but he has great diamonds with partner and good trumps. A Picture Jump to 3NT tells his tale well.

WEST	EAST
1♠	2◇
2♡	2♠
3NT	

Responder likes this development. He can count a likely eleven tricks in the form of five diamonds, five spades and the club ace. Trick 12 might easily come from a heart ruff. A fair risk exists, however, that diamonds are 4-1. If the opponents lead a trump and declarer plays a heart and another trump comes back, eleven tricks may be the limit, unless opener has the heart queen. Further, trumps may be a problem. Relying on two 3-2 splits might be too much. Thus, it seems useful to know if opener has the heart queen and/or the trump jack.

The first option is easiest — the 'Your Suit' asking bid, here 4♣. Since opener denied the ace and king of hearts with his 3NT call, he answers the Your Suit asking bid as if it were a Their Suit asking bid. Since he has the queen, he would answer positively, by bidding the second step, 4♡. Since 4♡ deprives responder of another cuebid below the next level in our suit (4♠) and is the best possible response, opener continues his answering by wrapping around with answers to a My Suit asking bid (the first of the remaining asking bid possibilities) and answers this question also.

The My Suit asking bid has modified responses when the Picture Jump to 3NT is used. They are parallel to the normal Your Suit asking bid responses, seeking the missing honor. Opener is missing the diamond ace (responder happens to know this already). Therefore, his response to the initial Your Suit asking bid is still 4♡. Had he held A-Q-x, he would have responded 4♠ (missing king); with A-K-x, he would respond 4NT (missing queen). Each shows the maximum Your Suit response — the queen — but clarifies the inferential My Suit asking bid.

Back to responder. He managed to ask two questions at once, accidentally — a neat trick. Of course, the secondary information was not helpful, because he already knew what opener's diamonds were. Had he held A-K-x of hearts and J-x-x-x-x of diamonds, though, this would have been useful. In any event, responder is now worried about the spade suit. The only remaining asking bid is the Our Suit asking bid — trumps. The Their Suit asking bid is dropped from the Picture Jump to 3NT structure as unnecessary.

Accordingly, responder bids 4NT. Opener has only two top honors and does not have the jack (the worst possible holding), so his response is 5♣. A conservative responder might now resign at 5♠. An aggressive responder might not care and go on to bid 6♠ anyway, but he could have skipped the trump asking bid if he was going to do this. Alternatively, responder may want to push a little more. Maybe opener has K-Q-10-x-x. That would help increase their chances in a small slam. Or maybe opener has the diamond jack. Logically, without discussion, 5♢ over 5♣ should suggest bidding slam if opener has the diamond jack. Bidding 5♡ instead would be a general 'Last Train' call, asking for something extra. On balance, 5♢ seems best. Once Yummy Toes asking bids are used up, suit calls by the captain (the person wielding the Yummy Toes asking bids) simply ask partner if he has something more to say about this particular suit.

If the 5♢ call is made, even without discussion, opener should understand that K-Q-J of diamonds is probably great stuff and bid 6♠. With no diamond jack and no trump ten, 5♠ seems automatic. The spade ten cannot be a bad card, however, and is perhaps enough to bid 5♡. This suggests that opener 'has' what responder would 'want' if responder had a chance to make a 'Last Train' call. A response of 5♡ would surely be understood and so the small slam would be bid in the belief that opener held K-Q-10-x-x of trumps.

You might object that all of this latter stuff is quite esoteric, at least after the asking bids have been exhausted. True, but in fact cuebidding is often esoteric. At times, after science is exhausted, the artistic side kicks in. This is where the partnership dance goes from a structured step to a whimsical dip. If your partner is on today, toss out the esoteric — you may be surprised at his fielding ability. If not, use your gut feelings.

The complete auction:

WEST	EAST
1♠	2◇
2♡	2♠
3NT[1]	4♣[2]
4♡[3]	4NT[4]
5♣[5]	5♠

or

5♣[5]	5◇[6]
5♠[7]	

1. Picture Jump to 3NT.
2. Your Suit (hearts) asking bid.
3. Positive (the queen), 'wrapped around' to also show K-Q-x of My Suit (no ace of diamonds — first step My Suit response).
4. Our Suit asking bid.
5. Only two top honors, without the jack.
6. Diamond jack? Or something extra?
7. No, and nothing else to show.

A final note on the Picture Jump to 3NT. When a major is agreed at the two-level, only one auction featuring a delayed Picture Jump to 3NT is possible:

WEST	EAST
1♡	2♣
2◇	2♡
2♠	3NT

As a result, there are no inferential mysteries to worry about with this call. You should note, though, that this Picture Jump to 3NT by responder does not necessarily imply a singleton spade — responder could be 2-3-3-5. Fortunately, the 2♠ call by opener makes this distinction less important. In this sole circumstance, responder should answer the Their Suit asking bid in spades by showing either the queen or a singleton as an 'I have it' answer. Thus, a Step One answer would show J-x or worse; a Step Two answer would show Q-x or singleton.

The Picture Jump to Game

We do not use fast arrival as the first action in a cuebidding sequence. What meaning, then, do we attach to the following auction?

WEST	EAST
1♠	2♣
2◊	2♠
4♠	

For us, despite apparent conventional wisdom, this is not an auction where opener is showing a dead minimum. A jump to game is only a signoff when partner has denied control in a suit in which the jumper might also lack control. In this auction, that is not possible.

If the Picture Jump to Game is the next call after a bid by partner has set the trump suit, then it shows a double-splinter hand, one that is, in other respects, parallel to a Picture Jump Cuebid. For example, consider:

WEST	EAST
1♠	2♣
2◊	2♠
4♠	

Opener's jump to 4♠ is used to show good trumps, great diamonds and two singletons, something like:

♠ A Q 8 7 5 2 ♡ 9 ◊ A Q J 6 5 ♣ 8

This is, admittedly, rare. Instead, a Picture Jump to Game is usually used as a catchall Picture Jump, covering any useful Picture Jumps not possible due to a lack of space for the jump.

If a Picture Jump to 3NT is not available by either opener or responder, then a Picture Jump to Game shows that holding and not the double single-ton option. If a Picture Splinter is not available, then the Picture Jump to Game shows that holding, not two singletons or the Picture Jump to 3NT option. Finally, if the only jump available is the Picture Jump to Game, it shows the same holding as the Picture Jump Cuebid.

Put another way, the Picture Jump to Game shows two singletons if all other Picture Jump options are available. If only some Picture Jumps are available, the Picture Jump to Game shows the 'most important' Picture Jump not available. The priority for this is:

(1)   the Picture Jump Cuebid
(2)   the Picture Splinter
(3)   the Picture Jump to 3NT

So, if the person jumping to game cannot be signing off, because there is no possible known lack of control in a suit, and if that person could not make a Picture Jump Cuebid (because there is not enough room to jump into his own suit), then the Picture Jump to Game shows the same pattern that is normally described by a Picture Jump Cuebid. Notice the caveat, which is important. In this auction:

WEST	EAST
1♡	2♣
2◇	2♡
2NT	4♡

East is simply confirming the lack of a spade control and signing off in 4♡.

The most common situation for the Picture Jump to Game would be when partner raises a minor response to a major opening. For example, consider the following auction:

WEST	EAST
1♠	2♣
3♣	4♠

Responder clearly bid 2♣ to set up a Picture Jump Cuebid. West's inconvenient raise ruined that plan, as 4♣ is no longer a jump. So responder simply jumps to 4♠.

If the person jumping to game cannot be signing off, because there is no known lack of control in a suit, and if that person could make a Picture Jump Cuebid but cannot make a Picture Splinter, then the Picture Jump to Game replaces the Picture Splinter. If the person so jumping to game could not make a Picture Splinter into either the side suit or partner's suit, we assume the side-suit splinter to be more important and, thus, to have priority.

A simple example of this principle:

WEST	EAST
1♠	2◇
2♡	2♠
3♣	4♠

Responder could, after 3♣, have made a Picture Cuebid of 4◇. However, he could not make a Picture Splinter in clubs after 3♣. Hence, 4♠ shows a Picture Splinter in clubs, the most important of the missing Picture Jumps. Note that a Picture Splinter to 4♡ is still possible.

The Picture Jump to Game might also be a delayed action, also covering the missing Picture Jump, by priority.

No Yummy Toes asking bids are used over the classic 6511 meaning.

An example of the simple Picture Jump to Game would have netted a making slam in the 2005 Farmen Invitational on this deal, where neither team found the slam:

WEST	EAST
♠ A K 8 6 4 2	♠ J 9 5
♡ K Q 10 9 4	♡ A 5
◇ 6	◇ K 8 7 4
♣ 2	♣ A Q J 10

West opened 1♠, East responding 2♣. West rebid 2♡ and both East players neglected to set trumps for some reason. Assuming a logical 2♠ from East, West is perfect for a Picture Jump to Game bid of 4♠, showing 6-5 pattern, two singletons and two of the top three honors in each of his suits.

This, of course, lets East in on most of the story. RKCB resolves the rest and 6♠ is bid. The slam probably makes whenever spades are 2-2, whenever the spade queen drops singleton or whenever North leads a trump or club and does not have the club king. A fair bet.

WEST	EAST
1♠	2♣
2♡	2♠
4♠	4NT
5♡	6♠

One final note is worth repeating and clarifying. A jump to game is not a signoff unless one's partner has denied control in a suit in which the jumper might also lack control. The other side of the coin is that a jump to game is definitely a signoff, and not a Picture Jump, whenever a specific and clear hole has been identified by partner and the jump bidder might not have the hole filled.

What does this mean? If partner has absolutely denied a club control, for example, then your jump to game in spades would be a signoff, probably because you do not have a club control either. If, however, partner showed a club control and has not denied anything else yet, then a jump to 4♠ by you would be a Picture Jump.

So if you jump to game or if you hear a jump to game, the first question should be whether any clear hole has been identified by one partner that might not be covered by the person jumping to game. If so, then the jump to game has a simple interpretation — slam is now hopeless. If not, then the jump to game must show something in particular, as we have discussed in this section.

TRUMP-SETTING PICTURE JUMPS

It's also possible to use a Picture Jump to set trumps by inference. When that Picture Jump establishes a major as trumps, the major can be thought as having been 'set' at the two-level. So the Picture Jump can be looked at as if it had been made after trumps had been set by partner at the two-level.

Picture Jumps in Support of the Second Suit

The most common use of Picture Jumps to agree trumps is to show, by default perhaps, a fit for opener's second suit. This is a space-saving technique, because the first suit bid by opener can be set most cheaply by a simple preference of the suit, usually at the two-level, whereas the second suit must be raised to the three-level. For example:

WEST	EAST
1♠	2♣
2♡	?

Responder could now make a Picture Jump to 4♣ or a Picture Splinter to 4◇ setting hearts — the second suit — as trumps. To establish spades as trumps, he would simply bid 2♠, possibly with a Picture Splinter to come later.

PICTURE SPLINTER INTO OPENER'S FIRST SUIT

An unnecessary jump below game into opener's first suit is defined, again by default, as a Picture Splinter, with support for the second suit. For example:

WEST	EAST
1♠	2♣
2♡	?

Responder could now jump to 3♠ to set hearts as trumps, to show a singleton spade, and to clarify the rest of the hand as described earlier for Picture Splinters.

THE PICTURE DOUBLE JUMP TO GAME

There are two exceptions to the rule that a Picture Jump shows support for the second suit. First, a jump to game in a major after opener bids a lower second suit is a Picture Jump Cuebid, showing support, with values in responder's first suit. I'll get to the second exception in a moment. An example:

WEST	EAST
1♠	2♣
2◇	4♠

Responder has something like:

♠ K Q 8   ♡ Q 7   ◇ 7 6   ♣ A Q J 6 5 4

This exception works because (1) this situation always involves a double jump and (2) a single jump would have been enough for a Picture Splinter.

There are a number of auctions in which a Picture Jump can be used to set trumps:

WEST	EAST
1♠	2♣
2♡	4♠

This 4♠ call would be a Picture Jump, functionally equivalent to a hypothetical auction where opener was able to raise responder in spades at the two-level. Spades are set as trumps 'at the two-level' in that the jump occurs when a two-level raise setting trumps could have been made.

This is an important idea to remember: a bid of 4♠ here is not simply a call that says that you have absolutely no slam aspirations. We do not make unilateral decisions of this nature. Partner is unlimited. There are few things as frustrating as having a hand in need of delicate analysis, only to have partner leap to 4♠ because he has a mere 13-count. Where? What honors? Why do you do this to me?

Perhaps in order to stop this annoying practice, I have defined this jump as a special call. Make it a convention, so partner can't do this to you anymore!

THE (OPTIONAL) PICTURE JUMP TO 3NT SETTING TRUMPS

The second possible exception (this should be discussed!) is the Picture Jump to 3NT when hearts is the agreed trump suit. Trust me for a minute that the reason this special bid applies only with hearts is to retain the ability to use 2♠ as a fourth-suit forcing call.

An example of this jump. Again, the auction is:

WEST	EAST
1♡	2♣
2♢	

If responder were to bid 3NT, under the definition described earlier, he would have something like:

♠ 6 5   ♡ K Q 2   ◊ A Q 7 6   ♣ Q 8 6 4

In other words, responder would have two-honor support for opener's second suit (diamonds), two honors and three-card help for opener's hearts and no controls on the side (with no inference of a singleton spade necessary). Obviously, this confirms heart support as well, as we use five-card major openings. In such circumstances, the politics of bridge suits, namely that majors are preferred citizens, justifies placing the focus on hearts. (You should note that this agreement requires an intermediate step of a 2NT call when no fit has been unearthed and responder wants to suggest 3NT as the final contract.)

As a result, the Picture Jump to 3NT requires support for hearts, but not necessarily length in opener's minor. Another example hand for this bid is therefore something like:

♠ 5 4   ♡ K Q 6   ◊ A Q 9   ♣ Q 9 8 6 2

In other words, the diamond 'fit' is secondary and not strictly necessary (other than the honors). Furthermore, hearts is the agreed suit for purposes of later cuebidding.

If this Picture Jump to 3NT to set trumps is used, then either 2♠ (fourth suit) or 2NT must be bid on any hand that would normally justify bidding 3NT.

This Picture Jump to 3NT is not used when spades are opener's first suit, for reasons that will be explained very shortly.

AFTER PICTURE JUMPS SETTING TRUMPS

As usual, Yummy Toes asking bids apply after either the fit-showing Picture Jump to 3NT or the Picture Jump to Game described in this section.

THE SPECIAL NON-JUMP 'JUMP' TO 3NT

One final, but important, note. Any raise of the 2NT cuebid (poor trumps) to 3NT is defined as a Picture Jump. This is a logical result of the impossibility of having nothing to cuebid between 2NT and 3NT and yet having serious slam interest. An example will explain this principle.

WEST	EAST
1♠	2♣
2◇	2♠
2NT	3NT

Without this agreement, 3NT would show serious slam interest without any possible cuebids or Picture Jumps. This is a logical impossibility. Thus, 3NT is defined as a Picture Jump, specifically a Picture Jump to 3NT.

If the agreed suit is hearts, opener just bypassed 2♠ as a cuebid; hence, he lacks a spade control. In this situation, the raise of 2NT to 3NT should also show second-round spade control.

Thus, this sequence

WEST	EAST
1♡	2♣
2◇	2♡
2NT	3NT

shows a spade control, while this one

WEST	EAST
1♡	2♣
2◇	3NT

(the sequence I discussed earlier) denies one.

When the agreed suit is spades, however, the delayed Picture Jump to 3NT would be redundant if an immediate jump to 3NT were a Picture Jump. You can see that responder is well placed to set up the delayed action when spades are trumps, as he is assured, by his own good trumps, that opener will bid 2NT over 2♠. Thus, it seems that a Picture Jump to 3NT for setting trumps should be used only when opener's first suit is hearts.

Special Jumps above Game

There are two types of jumps above game. One is a simple jump above game:

WEST	EAST
1♠	2♣
2◇	2♠
5♣	

The second is a jump above all asking bids, after partner has made a Picture Jump of some variety:

WEST	EAST
1♠	2♣
2◇	2♠
4♣	5◇

These calls are specialized Roman Keycard Blackwood asking bids.

A jump above game in a suit already shown is a Roman Keycard Blackwood call, with a twist. It refocuses the answers to have the key king and queen be the king and queen of the suit bid, not trumps.

An example. Suppose partner opens 1♠ and you hold:

♠ K Q 2   ♡ 5   ◇ A K   ♣ A 9 8 7 4 3 2

After you respond 2♣, partner rebids 2♡ and you bid 2♠, setting trumps. Suppose partner now cuebids 3♣.

WEST	EAST
1♠	2♣
2♡	2♠
3♣	?

You have a fair shot at slam and might even have a grand. Although a further cuebidding sequence might be beneficial, it could also get convoluted.

All you need to know about is the ace of spades, the ace of hearts and the secondary club honors. In this situation, you can jump to 5♣, Roman Keycard Blackwood, with partner showing the 'king of trumps', if he has the king of clubs, and the 'queen of trumps', if he has the queen of clubs. Neat tool, don't you think?

As I mentioned in the Introduction, I once witnessed a cuebidding sequence go wrong in the Vanderbilt where one of the partners held something like:

♠ A   ♡ A K Q 9 8   ◇ A 9 5 4 3 2   ♣ 3

After hearts were agreed as trumps, this player's partner cuebid a club control. Now a grand slam seemed plausible, but the partnership could never clarify the diamond situation. It seems to me that the simple solution would be a jump above game to 5◇, as described above. On this deal, his partner would have responded 6♣, showing two 'keycards', meaning the ace of clubs and the king of diamonds, as well as the 'queen of trumps', meaning the diamond queen, making the grand slam an easy call.

A jump above game into a suit where you could be short is Exclusion Roman Keycard Blackwood. For instance:

WEST	EAST
1♠	2♣
2◇	2♠
5♣	

This is a normal Roman Keycard Blackwood bid with the addition of a void in the suit bid, namely clubs. Partner is directed to ignore the club ace when counting his keycards. Opener might have something like:

♠ A K 7 5 3 2   ♡ 4   ◇ K Q 9 8 7 6   ♣ —

Unless discussed as specifically something else, any bid above game is treated as if it were a Jump, meaning RKCB of either an exclusionary or 'inclusionary' variety.

A Few Deals for Study

Let's end this part of the book by looking at some example deals and auctions to see how all these ideas work together in practice.

HAND 1

WEST	EAST
♠ A K 10 8 5	♠ Q 6 4
♡ Q 7 6	♡ A K 10 3
◇ A 6 5 4	◇ Q 8
♣ 3	♣ A J 10 8

The auction beings:

WEST	EAST
1♠	2♣
2◇	2♠
?	

Opener does not have the right hand for a Picture Jump. He has good trumps, so he bypasses 2NT. No club honor, so he bypasses 3♣ too. Only one diamond honor, so he bypasses 3◇. No heart control (first- or second-round), so he bypasses 3♡. Again, 3♠ is the option. As you can see, a direct raise of a major to the three-level after the major is set at the two-level in a game-forcing auction shows good trumps but nothing else. It does not show solid trumps.

Responder still has some fleeting hope of a slam. Suppose, for example, that opener has his best possible hand, namely:

♠ A K J 9 8   ♡ Q J 9   ◇ A J 5 4   ♣ 3

In that case, 6♠ seems icy.

So responder should bid 3NT, a serious slam try. This is not so much to show serious slam interest, but rather to assert that responder wants to assume captaincy and force cuebids from opener.

Opener can infer a lot from this call, but that is not necessary. Responder has taken control. Opener can be certain that responder has a heart control, of course.

WEST	EAST
1♠	2♣
2♦	2♠
3♠	3NT
?	

Opener can now cuebid 4♣. He has denied a club honor value, so logically this shows a club control in the form of shortness.

Responder gets more interested. Bidding 4♦ seems appropriate to show some help in diamonds, namely one of the top three honors.

Opener now bids 4♡. This is not Last Train, because opener is the puppet, showing his hand to partner, who claimed captaincy with the 3NT call. Opener must have third-round control in hearts, probably the queen.

WEST	EAST
1♠	2♣
2♦	2♠
3♠	3NT
4♣	4♦
4♡	?

Responder now feels somewhat safe moving on. An eleventh trick is available in most circumstances, so the five-level is not too risky. But responder needs more information. A call of 4NT (RKCB) would allow him to clarify that the diamond honor is the ace. However, it would tell him little about the depth needed for a slam. Bidding 5♡ would sound like Exclusion RKCB. On the other hand, he could have used that option directly over 4♦. On second thought, 5♡ could be an asking bid, seeking help in hearts for the slam. That might locate the heart jack, but then the diamond situation would be unknown.

5♦, similarly, cannot be Exclusion RKCB; after all, responder could have jumped to 5♦ as Exclusion directly over 3♠. Thus, 5♦ also sounds like an asking bid, seeking help in diamonds, logically the missing jack (the ace could be found with straight RKCB). However, in neither circumstance is it fair to toss partner such a strange switch of system. A five-level call in a side suit that could be short is Exclusion RKCB, period. So what can we do?

Wait a second. Over 4◇, 4♡ was the best possible bid from opener, so how could it induce a signoff? Realizing this, responder has a simple solution. If he bids 4♠, the auction must still be ongoing, ever so gently.

Note the principles at play here:

1. A five-level call in a side suit is normally assumed to be Exclusion RKCB. This is untrue only if the person making the call cannot have a void in that suit. If no void is possible, then the five-level call is RKCB, with the minor keycards converted to the side suit.
2. If the last cuebid below game is made by the partner of the person who bid Serious 3NT, this is a true cuebid, not Last Train.
3. If a true cuebid of the last suit below game is made as the only possible cuebid, partner's bid of game in the agreed suit is not a signoff. Instead, it shows mild slam interest.

This last principle is a rare occurrence, but let's run over it again with a concrete example. If spades are agreed as trumps, then after a Serious 3NT bid, partner might cuebid 4♣ next, followed by 4◇ from the Serious 3NT bidder, followed by 4♡ from his partner. 4♡ (from the person who did not bid Serious 3NT) is a true cuebid and not Last Train. However, it denies nothing. When this occurs, 4♠, next, would indicate mild slam interest (the 4♡ cuebid was not yet enough).

HAND 2

WEST	EAST
♠ A J 9 6 5	♠ K Q 10
♡ K 9	♡ 3
◇ K 10 7 5	◇ J 8 6 3
♣ K 10	♣ A Q 8 6 3

The auction starts the same as on Hand 1:

WEST	EAST
1♠	2♣
2◇	2♠

Note that responder should not bid 3♡ after 2◇, because this Picture Splinter would show diamond support. Although responder does happen to have diamond support (of sorts), responder wants to set spades as trumps.

Opener lacks the requirements for a Picture Splinter. Since he has poor trumps, lacking two of the top three honors, his next cuebid is 2NT.

Now responder would like to make a Picture Splinter of 4♡, but his hand is shy of that call by the jack of clubs. He contents himself with a simple 3♣, showing two top club honors.

Opener doesn't have two top honors in his second suit (diamonds), so he bypasses 3◇. He does, however, have a heart control, second-round, so he cuebids 3♡.

WEST	EAST
1♠	2♣
2◇	2♠
2NT	3♣
3♡	?

Responder is troubled by this call. Opposite opener's actual hand, slam is hopeless, of course. But, perhaps opener has something like:

$$♠ A J 8 3 2 \quad ♡ A 4 \quad ◇ A 8 4 3 \quad ♣ K J$$

Twelve tricks are easy opposite the ideal hand. Responder lacks the third high spade (still not shown), so he bypasses 3♠, but he does have serious slam interest, so he bids 3NT.

Now opener can cuebid 4♣ to show his club honor.

WEST	EAST
1♠	2♣
2◇	2♠
2NT	3♣
3♡	3NT
4♣	?

This interests responder greatly. Both black suits are solid at the top, but more work needs to be done before committing to RKCB. Responder's first decision is easy — he bypasses 4◇ to deny a diamond card. This tells the partnership that only one top diamond is held. Opener should be looking to see if he has the ace of diamonds in his hand.

Responder elects to bid 4♡, a Last Train call. This is not a cuebid, because he bid Serious 3NT earlier. He is the captain. The 4♡ bid, therefore, asks opener to evaluate his hand contextually.

Opener has no problems here. Two red aces would get movement, but two red kings get a fast signoff. With luck game will make…

HAND 3

WEST	EAST
♠ A K Q 9 3	♠ J 10 4
♡ 8 5 4 2	♡ A 6 3
◇ A K Q 4	◇ J 2
♣ —	♣ A K J 4 3

1♠	2♣
2◇	2♠
?	

Easy so far. Now over to opener.

Opener's hand is wrong for a Picture Splinter, so he starts with the simple cuebidding sequence. An immediate leap to 5♣ as Exclusion RKCB has little appeal, since the need to find out more about hearts is too compelling. With good trumps, no club honor and good diamonds, 3◇ is his cuebid.

Responder has a promising minimum. No picture jump is possible, so he simply cuebids 3♡, showing a heart control.

This interests opener greatly, but there is plenty of time yet. For now, 3♠ to show the third spade card does the trick. Although 5♣ keeps lurking in opener's mind, the heart situation still needs to be explored.

WEST	EAST
1♠	2♣
2◇	2♠
3◇	3♡
3♠	?

Responder also has slam interest. However, he is not 'serious' enough to seize captaincy. He knows that opener does not have the missing club queen, or opener would have cuebid 3♣ initially, even with the singleton queen. It seems best to be conservative and simply tell partner the missing information — 4♣, two top club honors.

Opener still has difficulties if he takes over. He needs tricks. The 4♣ call suggests duplication of values as a risk, but 4◊, showing a third diamond honor, seems a good continuation. Responder will recognize the power of opener's diamonds and spades and be able to ascertain the value of his club honors or lack thereof.

WEST	EAST
1♠	2♣
2◊	2♠
3◊	3♡
3♠	4♣
4◊	?

The 4◊ cuebid raises new captaincy interest from responder. He now knows that his diamond jack is a critical card, an extra trick. Counting five spades and four diamonds, added to his three top rounded suit cards, gets responder to an easy twelve tricks. Even a grand is possible if clubs can be established. Opposite something like

♠ A K Q 5 3   ♡ 9 8 7   ◊ A K Q 9   ♣ 3

7♠ probably makes, unless clubs are 5-2 with the queen protected. The ♡Q-J from partner would increase your options and chances. A fifth diamond would assure the grand. Even a sixth spade from opener is possible.

Responder might think more about opener's actual hand, the worst possible. Assuming a heart lead (probable), opener could win, ruff a club, cash a top spade from hand, small spade to the ten, ruff another club (high), draw trumps and cross to dummy's diamond jack to run clubs from the top. This line will work, so long as spades are 3-2 and clubs are either 4-4 or the queen comes down in three rounds. If this offers good enough odds as the worst-case scenario, 7♠ seems a fair bid.

What if responder wants to be cautious? What if he resigns himself to playing the grand only if opener holds extra length in diamonds or spades? The simple solution is to bid 4NT — a concept first introduced by the Italians in the Neapolitan and Blue Club systems. When 4NT is bid by responder and opener has (i) promised a specific number of keycards in trumps, (ii) promised a specific number of keycards in his second suit, (iii) denied an honor in responder's suit and (iv) denied a control in hearts, 4NT cannot be RKCB. That would make no sense. We already know what the answer has to be.

When the answer to what would normally be RKCB is predetermined by prior bidding, 4NT asks for features: contextually relevant good things. Holdings that make you smile. Whatever. Features.

If opener held a fifth diamond, that would be a feature, so he would bid 5◇ over 4NT. A good heart card, perhaps the queen, would be potentially useful: opener could bid 5♡ with the queen of hearts. As opener has not shown club shortness yet, that, too, might be of interest. Opener denied club length, so 5♣ would suggest that opener has a club singleton or void.

Even with none of these, a sixth spade would have value. With a good holding in trumps, opener could bid 6♠ or perhaps show a second useful feature with a jump above 5♠. In other words, opener might bid 6♣ over 4NT with a sixth spade and shortness in clubs. As a result, failure to make a value-holding jump suggests only five trumps.

On the actual deal, after 4NT from responder, opener should realize that this calls for 'neat stuff' bidding. He has no club jack, no fifth diamond, no heart card and no sixth spade, so he signs off in 5♠. Responder raises to 6♠ with some disappointment. At least we really sniffed for the grand...

HAND 4

WEST	EAST
♠ K J 10 8 5	♠ A Q 9
♡ K J	♡ A Q
◇ A K J 7 4	◇ 10 9 8 3
♣ Q	♣ J 10 5 4

Opener starts with 1♠. Responder has a problem, but 2♣ seems the least of evils. Opener has a simple 2◇ rebid and responder sets trumps with 2♠.

WEST	EAST
1♠	2♣
2◇	2♠

No Picture Jump for opener, again. With poor trumps, 2NT is his call. There will be time later to bid aggressively with trumps that include J-10.

Responder clearly has poor clubs and bypasses 3♣. He lacks a diamond honor and therefore bypasses 3◇. Bidding 3♡ shows his heart control.

WEST	EAST
1♠	2♣
2◇	2♠
2NT	3♡
?	

Opener can now bid 3♠. He denied good trumps, so 3♠ promises only one top honor. He could have held ♠J-10-9-3-2, you realize. We do, at least, suspect very highly that opener has a diamond control or 4♠ would probably have been his bid. However, opener might be hoping that responder has a singleton diamond as a control.

Responder has a difficult problem now. Opener has provided little more information than that he has K-x-x-x-x or longer in spades. Responder has interesting holdings, like the fourth diamond and the other two top spade honors, but not much else.

A leap to 5♣ by responder would be RKCB, with the keycards now switched to clubs. However, given his pathetic holdings in the minors, this won't tell responder what he needs to know anyway. Having denied a diamond card earlier, bidding 4◇ would suggest a diamond control in the form of shortness, clearly wrong. A signoff in 4♠ seems too weak and using Serious 3NT seems too strong. Perhaps responder should fudge by bidding 4♡. No, that would show first- and second-round control of hearts, which is clearly a lie. Ultimately, then, 4♠ has to be the call. Best to trust partner.

WEST	EAST
1♠	2♣
2◇	2♠
2NT	3♡
3♠	4♠
?	

Opener should think this through. Responder's 4♠ call was not a signoff based on inability to cover a hole shown by opener, since opener has been unable to show anything except his trump holding. Even that much was an improvement after his initial 2NT cuebid. Responder has denied a top honor concentration in clubs, which is a good thing opposite a singleton.

Responder must have at least two diamonds, because he did not show diamond shortness with a 4◇ call. Responder is known to have the heart ace. In addition, responder's failure to sign off directly over 2NT suggests some continuing slam prospects.

Constructing the worst possible hand for responder, opener visualizes:

♠ ? ? x   ♡ A Q   ◇ x x   ♣ J x x x x x

To get to a hand worth a game force, responder needs at least the ace of spades. The visualized worst hand becomes:

♠ A 3 2   ♡ A Q   ◇ 3 2   ♣ J 6 5 4 3 2

That is still not enough for a 2/1 GF, though. It quickly becomes obvious that responder must have the spade queen as well. Now, the worst hand is:

♠ A Q 2   ♡ A Q   ◇ 3 2   ♣ J 6 5 4 3 2

Opposite the worst possible hand, the five-level is not assuredly safe. Adding one diamond, for

♠ A Q 2   ♡ A Q   ◇ 4 3 2   ♣ J 5 4 3 2

does not make the slam 50-50. We really need 3-2 splits in both spades and diamonds, as well as the diamond queen onside. Only a 5-4 diamond secondary fit would suffice.

Thus, 4♠ should be passed, although on the actual hands the slam often makes. Cuebidding helps, and great cuebidding helps a lot, but some hands just cannot be bid to the ideal contract.

- 4 -

OTHER MAJOR-SUIT AUCTIONS

THE MAJOR IS AGREED AT THE THREE-LEVEL IN A 2/1 GF AUCTION

Until now, we have been looking at auctions where a major suit is agreed as trumps at the two-level in a game-forcing auction. This is our best-case scenario for slam exploration, since we have the maximum amount of space available for cuebidding. However, life isn't always kind to us. In fact, quite often in a 2/1 game-forcing auction, a major is not agreed until the three-level. This can occur in several circumstances. A few examples:

WEST	EAST		WEST	EAST
1♡	2♣ (GF)		1♡	2♣ (GF)
2♠	3♡		3♣	3♡

WEST	EAST		WEST	EAST
1♠	2♡ (GF)		1♠	2♢ (GF)
3♡			2♡	3♡

WEST	EAST		WEST	EAST
1♠	2♣ (GF)		1♠	2♢ (GF)
2♠	3♠		3♣	3♠

WEST	EAST		WEST	EAST
1♠	2♢ (GF)		1♠	2♢ (GF)
2NT	3♠		3♢	3♠

As far as possible, the same principles continue to apply to our cuebidding. However, we can draw fewer inferences from failures to use Picture Jumps, as fewer Picture Jumps are possible. Furthermore, these auctions often create different sources for inferences.

You should distinguish between agreeing the major at the three-level by raising the last-bid suit and taking a preference back to the first-bid suit. Picture Jumps are more frequent in the former case. Consider a few examples.

WEST	EAST
1♠	2◊
3♣	3♠

This is the preference scenario. Had responder made a jump over 3♣, this would show, by default, a fit for the last-bid suit, clubs. Hence, 4♡ would be a Picture Splinter with club support and 4◊ would be a Picture Jump Cuebid with club support. A jump to 4♠ is treated as natural (showing spades, not shortness); accordingly, the only Picture Jump showing spade support would be this Picture Jump to Game. When the only Picture Jump available is the Picture Jump to Game, remember that we default to using the priority meaning, namely the Picture Jump Cuebid. Hence, a 4♠ call in the example would be a spade-suit Picture Jump Cuebid, showing good trumps, great diamonds and no side control. Yummy Toes asking bids could follow.

WEST	EAST
1♠	2♣
2♡	3♡

This is the raise of the last-bid suit scenario. Responder had many options for making Picture Jumps here, as 2♠ (and 4♠) is reserved for showing spade support. In this auction, alternatives to 3♡ are a jump to 3NT (if so agreed), 4♣, 4◊ and 4♡ as a Picture Jump, a Picture Jump Cuebid, a Picture Splinter and a Picture Jump to Game respectively — all agreeing hearts as trumps. Even 3♠ would be a Picture Splinter, in support of hearts. Thus, bidding 3♡ greatly limits East's possible hand types. Note that if the Picture Jump to 3NT is not available (having been agreed as natural in such a sequence), then the Picture Jump to Game shows the meaning normally attributed to that call, as previously described (good trumps and good support, poor elsewhere).

WEST	EAST
1♠	2♣
2♠	3♠

Here, again, responder had the option of jumping to 4♣, 4◇, 4♡ or even 4♠. This opens up the possibility of two different Picture Splinters (either unbid suit).

Even if the partnership has agreed that 3NT can be used as a Picture Jump, the logic of the auction will force it to have natural meaning on occasion. If the 3NT bidder's partner has not shown a second suit, for example, then 3NT becomes a natural bid:

WEST	EAST
1♠	2♣
2♠	3NT

In the same way:

WEST	EAST
1♠	2♣
2NT	3♠

This is equivalent to the situation where opener rebids 2♠, because the 2NT call did not introduce a new suit. Again, 3NT by East would have been natural (thank goodness!).

WEST	EAST
1♠	2♣
3♣	3♠

Bidding 3♠ resets trumps to spades. Jumps over 3♣, except 4♠, would be in furtherance of a minor-suit slam. A bid of 4♠, therefore, would be a Picture Jump Cuebid. This makes sense, as responder can be viewed as the one actually raising clubs, opener's second suit. This is equivalent to the earlier example in which opener bids 3♣ as a new suit.

WEST	EAST
1♠	2♡
3♡	

Opener could have made a Picture Jump, although not to 3♠, 3NT or 4♠. These bids have different meanings. However, Picture Splinters are possible.

A special note on this auction: we do not bounce back and forth between majors as trumps, unless the last agreed major is perhaps not the best major for a fit. This means, generally, that a major agreement can be switched only when a 5-3 fit is converted to a 4-4 major fit.

In this example, responder cannot convert the heart fit back to spades (unless possibly at the slam level). Thus, after 3♡, 3♠ should be a cuebid, not an attempt to change trumps back to spades. A bid of 4♠ over 3♡, very strange indeed, should be taken as the sole manner of returning to spades, a Picture Splinter showing concentrated values and 4-5-2-2 pattern. I expect 4♠ in this auction to be based on something like:

♠ A Q 5 2　♡ K Q J 8 7　♢ 3 2　♣ Q 8

This specific sequence

WEST	EAST
1♠	2♡
3♡	3♠

has been the start of a lot of problem auctions. It has also been the subject of a lot of controversy. Many feel that 3♠ should expose a double fit and not be bid unless responder holds three-card support for spades. This view troubles me. When the auction starts

WEST	EAST
1♠	2♡
3♡	

it is often critical to slam prospects that responder has help for opener's first suit. Give opener ♠A-Q-J-3-2, for example, and if responder holds ♠K-5, the spades will likely produce five tricks, with no finesse needed. Change responder's spades to ♠6-5 and now the spades produce five tricks only when the finesse works and the opponents' spades are split 3-3.

If responder cannot bid 3♠ after his hearts are raised because he doesn't have three spades, the result is that spades cannot be cuebid by either partner below 4♡. Thus, although spade solidity is perhaps one of the most critical issues for slam assessment, it is the one cuebid unavailable to either partner. From where I sit, allowing responder to clarify the spade situation with honor doubleton, or even a singleton honor, seems much more effective than having 3♠ promise a true double fit. This treatment is not unreasonable, as I would guess that those who bid 3♠ to show a double fit require no top honor in spades for that call, perhaps being willing to bid 3♠ on ♠J-3-2 or even three small.

Since holding a spade card, fit or no fit, is so critical to a heart slam, and since there is no opportunity for either partner to cuebid spades below 4♡ except 3♠, I very strongly suggest the 'controversial' treatment that 3♠ simply be a cuebid and not establish a double fit. Hearts are agreed: end of story.

Finally, what about the auction where four suits are bid?

WEST	EAST
1♠	2♣
2♢	2♡

If opener makes a jump now (other than to 3NT), logically, it should be in support of hearts. Therefore, bidding 3♡ would imply an inability to make a Picture Jump. (As opener cannot have more than a singleton club, 3NT could not logically show a Picture Jump meaning, which promises three clubs with two honors. Thus, 3NT in this auction would simply show a dead minimum with no fit.)

When the auction involves many Picture Jump options, the most important cuebids forfeited are the 2NT 'poor trumps' cuebid and the parallel 'good trumps' cuebid of our major at the three-level. This affects inferences, of course, but information may still be inferred from cuebidding and from failure to make a Picture Jump. When Picture Jumps are of limited availability, even fewer inferences are available.

In these circumstances, you should resort to general principles rather than focusing on fine-tuning. As trump quality is always critical, special consideration of this problem should be an active part of your decision-making.

These factors affect the Serious 3NT meaning.

Consider the following example. You open 1♠ with:

♠ K Q 5 4 3 ♡ A 10 ♢ J 9 7 6 ♣ K 5

Partner responds 2♣, setting up a game force, and you bid 2NT (you believe that the diamonds are too ugly to mention). Partner now sets trumps with 3♠.

WEST	EAST
1♠	2♣
2NT	3♠
?	

You still don't know much about partner's hand. Clearly, he could not have made any Picture Jumps — his trumps aren't good enough. So what is your next call after 3♠?

A simple analysis suggests that this mere 13-count should be handled with a 4♣ bid to show non-serious slam interest and a club control, probably of interest to partner. If partner now bids 4◊, showing a diamond control, you can bid 4♡ to show a heart control. Partner should use his judgment from here on, right? No! Thinking that would be dead wrong.

Remember, a key problem with this cramped auction is that the quality of the spade honors cannot be shown. When you hold good trumps in a cramped cuebidding sequence, you should generally consider making a Serious 3NT call. But this is a 13-count, right? How can you possibly consider showing serious slam interest?

Think through what partner knows of your hand. Assuming that you would open 1NT with a five-card major, responder should visualize your 2NT call as showing either 11-14 HCP or 18-19 HCP. With 18-19 HCP opposite a hand on which partner has forced to game, you will undoubtedly pursue slam, unless a control problem comes to light. This is not a hand type where you need assistance from partner, at least not much.

So the difference between a courtesy cue and a Serious 3NT call should distinguish a bad minimum (11-12) with poor trumps on the low end from a good maximum (13-14) with good trumps on the high end, with middling hands judged accordingly. Thus, you are 'serious' about slam exploration since you have the maximum type of hand that is contextually possible, with which you would not take control yourself. In other words, you are 'serious' because you have the best possible cooperative hand. Let's look at what you actually have:

♠ K Q 5 4 3   ♡ A 10   ◊ J 9 7 6   ♣ K 5

Your hand qualifies initially as a high-end minimum, i.e. 'serious' interest. You have good trumps (K-Q) and a maximum (13-14 HCP). Further, you have a good holding in clubs and first-round control of hearts. Sure,

$$♠ K Q 10 9 8 \quad ♡ A 6 \quad ◇ 10 9 8 7 \quad ♣ K Q$$

would be the best possible hand, but four controls and the trump queen are nothing to sneeze at. In contrast,

$$♠ K Q 5 3 2 \quad ♡ K 3 \quad ◇ J 10 7 4 \quad ♣ K J$$

looks much worse.

The parameters for this type of 'serious' 3NT bid should be discussed by your partnership, as it comes up quite frequently. I would suggest that the following auction

WEST	EAST
1M	2suit
2NT	3M
3NT	

be precisely defined as either 18-19 HCP or 12-14 with two top honors in trumps, an ace in one of the side suits and either the king or ace in responder's suit or a second side ace. If opener had the ability to bid 3♠ (when hearts are the agreed fit) and did not, then 3NT must show, in the case of the 12-14 option, the other minor ace and help for responder's minor. Some examples follow.

WEST	EAST
1♠	2♣
2NT	3♠
3NT	

Opener might have:

$$♠ A Q x x x \quad ♡ x x x \quad ◇ A x x \quad ♣ K x$$

$$♠ K Q x x x \quad ♡ A x x \quad ◇ A x x \quad ♣ x x$$

$$♠ K Q x x x \quad ♡ A x x \quad ◇ x x x \quad ♣ K Q$$

$$♠ A Q J x x \quad ♡ A Q x \quad ◇ K Q x \quad ♣ x x$$

WEST	EAST
1♡	2♢
2NT	3♡
3NT	

Opener cannot have a spade control or he would have bid 3♠. So, we can expect one of the following hands:

♠ Q x   ♡ K Q x x x   ♢ K x   ♣ A x x x

♠ Q x x   ♡ A Q x x x   ♢ A K x   ♣ K x

You may protest that responder can't possibly handle these wildly divergent holdings. This is not a serious problem. Responder should assume the weaker holdings — the 'great minimums' — when assessing slam. In other words, 3NT in this context is assumed to show seriously cooperative values. If opener actually has the 18-19 count, he will not sign off and will not respect a signoff suggestion.

The idea of what could be called 'Two-Way Serious 3NT' might be disturbing for some readers. The problem is in the concept of captaincy. Usually, a Serious 3NT call establishes the person making the 3NT call as the presumptive 'captain' of the auction, with his partner telling more of the tale to enable the captain to decide the partnership's destination. When a Serious 3NT call shows either a 'perfect minimum' or a balanced 18-19 count, captaincy is, in a sense, undetermined. Responder should assess first whether the perfect minimum is enough for slam. If it is, then responder has no problem. If responder needs clarification of which perfect minimum opener has, continuing the cuebidding sequence should clarify matters. If opener happens to hold the 18-19 count, then the hand surely suffices in lieu of the perfect minimum.

If responder determines that the perfect minimum is not sufficient, he makes purely cooperative cuebids en route to a planned signoff. If opener hears such a cuebid and holds the 18-19 balanced hand, the information may be enough to launch him into asking for keycards or he might decide to sign off.

Keep in mind that the call made is the same whether the cuebid is cooperative or investigatory. The only difference between a person who cooperates and one who is captain lies in the purpose of their cuebids. A captain-like cuebid from responder will be of high importance to opener even if it is opener who is truly the captain, because his hand is the 18-19 count.

This scheme results in one of four possibilities. It may be that each partner makes cooperative cuebids for the other, never planning any action above game themselves. Alternatively, either opener or responder might be acting as an unannounced but interested party, never revealing that interest unless and until launching past game. In either event, the other partner is merely cooperating, waiting with great interest to see whether these cuebids are for a purpose or just for practice. Finally, both partners might be interested. If so, life is good, and this will be known when one partner surprises the other by taking off past game.

AFTER A NON-FORCING MAJOR-SUIT RAISE TO THE TWO-LEVEL

When responder raises a major suit to the two-level, slam seems remote. Consider this simple auction:

WEST	EAST
1♠	2♠
?	

Even if 2♠ shows constructive values, we know responder is limited to a maximum of about 10 HCP, with no great trump support — indeed, only minimal three-card support if some variety of Bergen Raises is used. Opener is also limited to a maximum of about 21 HCP. Thus, we know that any slam will have to be based on shape and fit.

Cuebidding in this situation is secondary to game tries. However, a common failing of many players and many partnerships in 'game try' auctions is to forget that opener may have slam try intentions. Catering to that possibility is important.

Again, remember that a slam in this context must be based on distribution. Opener may have relatively weak high-card strength, but excellent playing strength. It seems appropriate to distinguish these hand types with a reasonable game-try structure.

I have tried many of the multi-method game-try structures and I find the simplest to be the most effective. The following structure will be assumed throughout these discussions.

1. 2NT is a general invitation, a quantitative game bash. While it does not specifically invite responder to propose 3NT as a viable contract, it is a required bid before the partnership can play in 3NT.

2. Suit calls, in contrast, are game tries showing a second suit (presumably) and rule out 3NT as a viable suggestion by responder, converting any 3NT call to (contextually) serious.

The 'game try' can be shown to be a slam try if followed by a call that must logically be a move toward slam. The same general rules concerning cuebidding in game-forcing auctions play out, except that Picture Jumps and Splinters are different (must be stronger perforce). Responder should also cater to slam tries. The easiest way to explain these concepts is with example auctions.

THE SERIOUS 3NT BY RESPONDER

This situation seems absurd, right? Responder has limited his hand to about 8-11 HCP. How can he ever be 'seriously' interested in slam?

Consider a real auction:

WEST	EAST
1♠	2♠
3♦	？

Responder assumes that opener is making a game try. However, if he can accept the game try, he will cuebid as if opener were making a slam try.

Imagine two hands where responder might accept:

♠ K Q 2 ♡ 5 4 2 ♦ K Q 7 5 ♣ 8 6 5

♠ K J 2 ♡ A 2 ♦ Q 2 ♣ 9 8 7 6 4 2

On the first hand, responder can almost visualize a slam himself. Give opener something like:

♠ A 7 5 4 3 ♡ 10 ♦ A J 8 6 4 ♣ A 2

On these cards, 6◇ looks a fine spot. Pair this with the second hand and slam seems a tad more distant. The key seems to be the secondary fit.

Even with the second hand, slam is possible. Give opener something stronger, like

$$\spadesuit \text{A Q 7 5 4} \quad \heartsuit \text{9 3} \quad \diamondsuit \text{A K J 8} \quad \clubsuit \text{A 5}$$

and 6♠ seems fairly viable. The second hand, however, needs an opener with complementary slam interest.

What, then, should responder do to clarify his holding?

With the first hand, responder should bid 3NT in response to 3◇. This shows serious slam interest, meaning at least three of the top six honors in the two suits bid by opener, with a fit for the second suit. In fact, responder may well have greater interest in the second suit.

With the second hand, responder should accept the game try without showing serious slam interest. He does this by cuebidding naturally. His call, therefore, would be 3♡, showing a heart card, ostensibly a further game try. If opener now bids 3NT (Serious), responder can cuebid 4◇, showing a diamond card (one of the top three honors) and denying a club control.

This structure is different from the one you might expect. People normally raise the second suit to show a hand with a fit for the second suit. The reason for this special 3NT call as an alternative is to enable a cute treatment: 4♣ after responder's Serious 3NT should be Last Train, a general slam try for the new suit.

So what about after the following auction?

WEST	EAST
1♠	2♠
3◇	3NT
?	

Opener can now bid 4♣ as Last Train, establishing diamonds as the trump suit.

Consider how preferable this is, especially when the second suit is hearts after a spade fit is found.

WEST	EAST
1♠	2♠
3♡	?

A 4♡ bid leaves no space to consider slam. We know of the secondary fit, but no more, with no space left for exploring the slam potential. However, if responder bids Serious 3NT in response to a new suit call and if opener bids 4♣ as a Last Train call for the newly agreed suit, then responder, with four 'cover cards', can 'accept' the 4♣ call. Cover cards are defined as any of the top three honors in either the major or the second suit or both, as well as any outside ace.

The responses are as follows:

Four of the Major	Only three cover cards
Cheapest Bid in a New Suit	Three cover cards, plus the king of the suit bid
Six of the Second Suit	Four cover cards

An example:

WEST	EAST
1♠	2♠
3♣	3NT
4♣	?

With his 3NT call, responder has raised clubs, with serious interest. Opener has explored slam by bidding 4♣. Responder would answer as follows:

4◊	=	Perhaps ♠ Q 5 3 ♡ 8 6 5 ◊ K 3 2 ♣ K Q 9 7
4♡	=	Perhaps ♠ Q 5 3 ♡ K 9 7 6 ◊ 6 5 ♣ K Q 5 4
4♠	=	Perhaps ♠ K 4 2 ♡ 7 6 3 ◊ 9 8 7 ♣ A Q 7 6
6♣	=	Perhaps ♠ K Q 8 ♡ 6 5 4 3 ◊ 6 5 ♣ K Q 4 2

One note on this, however. What if the auction is:

WEST	EAST
1♡	2♡
2♠	?

Responder should now bid 3♠ to show a spade raise with serious slam interest. Never bypass a spade raise in order to bid 3NT. Why? Because 2♠ is the one new-suit call that might be based on a fragment, exploring for 3NT. Bidding 3NT immediately would show game-acceptance with interest in 3NT (notwithstanding the general rule that 3NT is not viable

after a new-suit call). If the bidding goes as shown, opener might be seeking 3NT and bidding the one feature he can show below 2NT. After 2♠
is raised to 3♠, opener can reject the new suit by bidding 3NT or 4♡; any
other call agrees spades and is a cuebid, except that 4♣ is an asking bid, as
if responder had bid Serious 3NT over 3♠.

Consider another two hands for responder after a 3◇ game/slam try:

WEST	EAST
1♠	2♠
3◇	?

♠ K 5 4   ♡ A 9 8   ◇ Q 9 7 6   ♣ 8 7 6

♠ K J 7   ♡ K J 7   ◇ Q 8 7 5   ♣ 10 7 2

On the first hand, responder has a fit for the new suit and three or more
cover cards (a side ace is a cover card). He lacks body, but the hand is still
strong and he should bid 3NT.

Opposite

♠ A 9 8 3 2   ♡ 3 2   ◇ A K J 8   ♣ A 9

slam will not make, but the special 4♣ call will resolve this problem.

Holding

♠ A Q 9 8 3   ♡ 3 2   ◇ A K J 8   ♣ A 9

however, opener can pretty much bid the slam without even asking questions.

With

♠ A Q 9 3 2   ♡ 2   ◇ A K J 8   ♣ A 9 2

opener could certainly bid the grand without asking any questions.

With

♠ A Q 9 8 3   ♡ —   ◇ A K J 8 2   ♣ 8 7 6

however, opener needs to know the precise location of the side ace(s), which
4♣ will supply.

On the second hand, the HCP count is higher, but the slow heart values deprive responder of three controls. Bidding 3♡, non-serious, works better.

Let's go to extremes. Suppose responder wants to bid a flier game in the second suit when it is hearts. We need him to be able to raise to game with this hand. Thus, after the following auction,

WEST	EAST
1♠	2♠
3♡	?

responder is permitted to raise to 4♡. This denies holding three assured cover cards. That is very weak, of course, but responder might want to take a flier on a prayer. This usually features a side doubleton or a side singleton with few key honors.

How about the high end? Responder is permitted to make a Picture Splinter on an appropriate hand. Suppose, for instance, that responder holds:

♠ Q 3 2   ♡ 5   ♢ K Q 9 8 5   ♣ 7 6 4 3

A simple raise of 1♠ to 2♠ seems fair. Now, if opener bids 3♢, responder could easily justify a jump to 4♡, showing a singleton heart, a diamond fit and three cover cards.

Alternatively, responder might opt for a slower showing of a singleton, especially if he thinks it advisable to first find out how serious opener is about slam. Thus, after responder's 3NT and opener's 4♣ asking bid, any jump in a new suit would also be a Picture Splinter. A bid of 4NT would be a Picture Splinter for clubs if some other suit is agreed.

Look at the following auction:

WEST	EAST
1♠	2♠
3♢	3NT
4♣	?

Responder's 3NT showed good diamond support. Opener's 4♣ agreed diamonds (for slam) and asked for more information. The responses are as follows:

4NT	Splinter in clubs, three cover cards
Four of the Major (4♠)	Only three cover cards
New Suit (4♡ or 5♣)	Three cover cards, plus the king of the suit bid
Jump to 5♡	Splinter (better to bid 4♡ over 3◇, directly), three cover cards
Six of the Second Suit (6◇)	Four cover cards

A FOUR-CARD MAJOR IS RAISED TO THE TWO-LEVEL

This circumstance, if it is a raise by responder, occurs in only one type of auction. Opener starts with a minor, hears a suit response, rebids one of a major and that major is raised. If a Walsh style of responses is used, where diamonds are generally bypassed by responder with a weak hand, this occurs in only two auctions:

WEST	EAST
1♣	1♡
1♠	2♠

and

WEST	EAST
1◇	1♡
1♠	2♠

The principles of cuebidding in this auction resemble those after the simple major raise. However, opener is suspected to have a long minor (5+). Logically, this creates the ability for opener to make a Picture Jump Cuebid or a Picture Splinter, and to cuebid a suit that has been previously shown.

Let's stop and think for a moment about the Picture Jump Cuebid in this type of auction, with responder severely limited. One can hardly justify a jump like this on 5422 pattern and no side stoppers, unless the minor and major are solid or semi-solid. Hence, analyze this auction:

WEST	EAST
1♣	1♡
1♠	2♠
4♣	?

I expect opener to use this Picture Jump to show something like

$$♠ A K Q 2 \quad ♡ J 4 \quad ◇ 9 2 \quad ♣ A K J 9 6$$

possibly changing the spade queen to the club queen.

If responder's major is raised to the two-level, we have a unique sequence. Although no game-force has yet been established, responder is virtually unlimited and potentially very strong. Accordingly, opener should be very active in cuebidding when accepting what is purportedly a game try, but which may be revealed later as a slam try.

For example, consider this simple auction:

WEST	EAST
1◇	1♡
2♡	?

If responder now bids 3♣, opener should assume that responder is making a game try. However, responder could have 20 HCP in this auction and 3♣ may be a prelude to a slam auction. Opener is also allowed to make a Serious 3NT call, as in any major-suit cuebidding auction. Opener would probably have something approaching a six-loser hand, with some kind of club fit.

Some Additional Comments

A few suggestions and tips for cuebidding sequences are worth noting.

First, if you are playing 2/1 GF, you should often bid 2♣ in response to partner's opening, whatever it is, in order to create a low-level game force. This may enable partner to make another call at the two-level and allow a lower setting of trumps and, accordingly, cheaper cuebidding. For example, a response of 2♣ to a 1♡ opening, holding

$$♠ A J 6 2 \quad ♡ 9 7 6 \quad ◇ A 10 2 \quad ♣ A K 4$$

might work out well. The greatest risk is a 3♣ rebid from opener, which forfeits nothing. If partner can bid 2◇, however, we gain an entire level. Bidding 1♠ simply causes too much confusion later if trying to get back to hearts and makes it harder to create a game force.

Second, and related to this first theme, you should consider making your initial response in a good fragment in order to enhance cuebidding. Let's look at the prior example again.

♠ A J 6 2   ♡ 9 7 6   ◇ A 10 2   ♣ A K 4

Since you have two of the top three honors in clubs, bidding 2♣ over 1♡ enables you to cuebid clubs later and show both honors at once. It also allows partner to cuebid the missing club queen for you. Bidding diamonds, by contrast, deprives you of the ability to cuebid your control in diamonds and makes it easy for partner to cuebid the diamond queen, which is not helpful. Thus, even with a more radical

♠ A J 8   ♡ 9 3 2   ◇ A 9 8 4   ♣ A K 4

I like a 2♣ response to 1♡, because of the way it facilitates later cuebidding.

Third, tend to set up the game-forcing auction rather than responding 1♠. Tactics often dictate which response to make.

An example that illustrates two of these suggestions comes from the 2005 World Championships Seniors Bowl. One team reached 7NT on this deal; the other stopped at game in spades. The hands are rotated:

WEST	EAST
♠ A K 8 6 4	♠ Q J 2
♡ A 6 5	♡ K Q J 7
◇ A Q 7	◇ K
♣ 9 8	♣ A Q 10 6 5

West opens 1♠ and hears a 2♣ response. With such a powerhouse hand, they are headed toward a slam and opener can take some liberties. The 'standard' rebid is 2NT, but 2◇ offers two great possibilities. First, responder might be planning to set spades as trumps. In that event, 2◇ saves an entire level of bidding. Second, opener may very well be able to cuebid the diamond suit and show his hand better after choosing a 2◇ rebid.

This decision to rebid 2◇ pays off when responder does, in fact, agree spades with 2♠. Now opener can bypass 2NT (good trumps), bypass 3♣ (no club honor) and cuebid 3◇ (two of the top three honors in diamonds. Responder will now cuebid 3♡, which allows opener to complete his honor description by cuebidding 4♡. This denies a third spade honor, denies serious slam interest (within the context of what he will be showing), denies a club shortness control (with honors denied, a late 4♣ should show a shortness control), denies a third diamond honor (no 4◇ cuebid) and shows a heart control, all of which describes opener's hand perfectly.

East can now continue with 4NT RKCB to clarify the heart control (shortness or the ace). When he hears four keycards, he can count thirteen tricks. 7NT is easy.

Note the importance of the 2◇ bid. By declining to bid 2NT, West kept the auction lower, which allowed West to describe his hand completely, including showing the diamond queen. Hearing about the diamond queen let East know that his diamond king, albeit singleton, was a huge card.

If West bids 2NT instead, East is forced to bid 3♠ to establish the spade fit. West would then bid 3NT, which could be the Serious 3NT variety of a control-rich maximal minimum. The auction thereafter is preempted, such that delicate exploration of the grand slam will be difficult at best.

- 5 -

MINOR FITS AFTER A MAJOR OPENING, 2/1 GF

In the normal course of events, the minors get tossed to the end of the line, bullied and rejected. However, we all love it when the underdog comes through. So we love finding that well-fitting minor-suit slam no one else in the field sniffs, while they subside in 3NT. Even better is the minor-suit grand slam! Accordingly, there is room for discussion of this grandest of dreams.

One issue in the exploration of minor-suit slams is that the old notrump contract keeps butting its head in. After all, 3NT certainly sounds like a great place to end when the minor slam is ruled out. Even 4NT, especially at matchpoints, sounds lovelier than 5♣, especially if both make. Even 5NT, although an ugly contract, might be the last chance to bail on an abandoned minor-slam exploration.

Another problem with minors is that even a raise might not set the trump suit affirmatively. If a slam is to be bid, perhaps 6NT will be the best spot. Even another suit, one of those arrogant majors, might ultimately win the day. How often do you open a major, hear partner's minor, gleefully raise that minor and then almost hear a sigh of disappointment from the minor as partner returns to your major?

Yet another problem with minors is that responder has the right to lie about a minor holding, and he often indulges himself in that privilege. Both 2♣ and 2♢, as responses to a major-suit opening, are often 'made up' bids. This creates a problem, in a sense, because even a bid and raise of a minor might have failed to locate a viable fit, let alone the best strain.

Cuebidding in minor-suit auctions is thus troubled by the constant intrusion of major-suit and notrump contracts. As a result, much is lost in the way of Picture Jumps, cuebids, special treatments and the like. There is no 'Serious 3NT' after a minor suit is agreed. Rather, it is replaced by a lot of confusing either-or bids, ambiguities and plain guesses. I will attempt to explain my best guess as to how the experts think, or should think, about these sequences.

MINOR FIT 'AGREED' AT THE THREE-LEVEL

After a major opening, there are only a few auctions in which a minor-suit fit can be found by the three-level in a 2/1 GF auction. The simplest two instances are where a response of 2♣ or 2♦ is raised to 3♣ or 3♦ respectively. As mentioned earlier, this does not really confirm a fit, as responder's 2♣ or 2♦ may have been a 'convenient' response with game-forcing values and no other option besides bidding a three-card minor. A related auction is the following:

WEST	EAST
1♡/1♠	2♣
2♦	3♦

Likewise, there are merits to a fragmentary 2♦ rebid by opener on some hands. He hopes to save space if partner really holds a fit for his major.

A minor suit might also be 'raised' with a preference call. This occurs if responder starts with 2♦ and then bids 3♣, and opener gives preference back to 3♦. The sequence at least establishes a true fit.

A delayed raise might also establish a minor 'fit'. Consider this example:

WEST	EAST
1♠	2♣
2♡	2NT
3♣	

Opener might easily have 5-4-0-4 pattern and bid 2♡, just because 'hearts is a major suit'. Even if partner is 5-4-1-3, your 2NT call usually features a five-card minor, unless you are specifically 2-3-4-4. Thus, a delayed minor raise like this usually, but not always, establishes a real fit.

In any event, cuebidding is limited for the minors, as major-suit strains might still be sought and notrump viability might be the pressing issue. Some Picture Jumps are possible, however, which helps.

In the following sections, I discuss each specific type of minor-suit agreement at the three-level.

AFTER A DIRECT RAISE OF RESPONDER'S MINOR

Consider this auction:

WEST	EAST
1♠	2♣
3♣	?

Responder can set spades as trumps by bidding 3♠. Any other call essentially agrees clubs as the focus suit. However, a minor focus suit does not mean that the best game is five of that minor — 3NT is often superior, despite a minor-suit fit.

In such an auction, a new suit cuebid below 3NT is an 'either-or' bid. Opener should assume that the call is made in pursuit of 3NT, showing a feature and suggesting the need for help in the remaining suit. For instance, bidding 3◊ in the sample auction should be treated initially as showing interest in playing 3NT, a diamond feature and a problem in hearts.

Opener will bid accordingly. Unless he has slam interest in that minor himself, he should bid 3NT with hearts under control. Any other call by opener suggests slam interest, except returning to the minor at the four-level, which merely shows lack of a heart control and no personal slam interest.

If responder was moving towards slam, the 3NT call by opener at least indicates values in hearts, which may help the exploration. Usually, the fourth-suit value is the ace or king, but Q-J-10-(x) is possible. In any event, responder will show that the initial new suit was actually meant as a slam-going cuebid by continuing beyond 3NT.

Let's go back to our example auction:

WEST	EAST
1♠	2♣
3♣	?

If responder now bids 3♡, say, this is initially taken by opener as a probe for 3NT, asking for diamond help. If opener has no independent interest in a slam, but has diamonds under control, he bids 3NT. Responder can now cuebid 4♣, which clarifies that 3♡ was really meant as a cuebid (first or second-round control of hearts).

We are now at 4♣. Before going further, we should explore the issue of the ace-asking bid in minor-suit slam auctions.

RKCB FOR A MINOR

Using 4NT as the keycard-asking bid in minor-suit auctions has obvious problems: it takes up a lot of space; it's easy to get too high and we have little or no room for queen or king asks over the response. So, when one minor has been agreed as the strain, use four of the cheaper 'out-of-focus' major as the RKCB asking bid. In the example auction we have been discussing, West opens 1♠. No one bids hearts. Therefore, 4♡ cannot be deemed a possible contract. Accordingly, 4♡ is defined as RKCB for the agreed minor.

BACK TO CUEBIDDING

Cuebidding in support of minor suits will seem strange. For major suits, the decision point seems to be four of the trump suit. You generally do not want to bypass four of the major unless you are commencing some form of ace-asking. Accordingly, Last Train is a treatment used to make one last check for something before bypassing the four-level.

Minors are different: if you want to make use of RKCB, you can do it below game in the minor. Thus, to a degree, you can feel somewhat free to ask for aces whenever you want, as long as the higher responses will not force you into a non-making slam. Even then, you might still ask if you are willing to sign off in 5NT.

In any event, the decision point in a minor-slam auction is not only just below the game level. Rather, it is also at the point where the out-of-focus major would be bypassed. Thus, there seem to be two places where 'Last Train' thinking could occur: the lowest cuebid below the RKCB bid, and the lowest cuebid below five of the agreed minor.

Also strange is that one might cuebid past the out-of-focus major without bypassing five of the minor. For example, if diamonds are trumps, and 4♠ is the RKCB bid, 5♣ could easily be a cuebid. This would be done if, for instance, the cuebidding alternative might give partner more useful information than you would get by asking partner for aces.

Let's look at some examples.

WEST	EAST
1♠	2♣
3♣	3◇
?	

Responder either has interest in a 3NT contract or is making a cuebid in a slam exploration. Suppose opener bids 3NT, showing control of hearts for notrump purposes. If responder now bids 4♣, we know a few things:

Responder's 3◇ call was actually a cuebid, seeking a slam.

Opener has inadvertently bid 3NT as non-serious, with values in hearts.

4♡ has become the RKCB bid, since it is the out-of-focus major.

Responder had two cuebids available below the RKCB bid.

If anything is a Last Train call, it would be 4◇ (one below 4♡, the out-of-focus major). So, we can surmise that 4♣ is a true cuebid. Since a true cuebid in the trump suit shows two of the top three honors, we know that responder has two top club honors.

What if responder had bid 4◇ instead? Last Train makes sense here. Since 4♣ would have been a true cuebid, we know that responder does not have two of the top three trump honors. So, we can interpret responder's options as 4♣ as a slam try with good trumps and 4◇ as a slam try with poor trumps.

Opener now has three options. If responder's cuebid told the tale and RKCB makes sense, opener can bid 4♡. If opener has no interest in slam, he can logically sign off in 4NT or 5♣, the two most viable contracts. With continuing slam interest but a preference for showing, opener could opt to continue cuebidding with 4♦ (after 4♣) or 4♠.

WEST	EAST
1♠	2♣
3♣	3♦
3NT	4♣
?	

Note that there should not be a minor-suit auction where both partners can make a Last Train bid. If responder could have made a Last Train bid, then opener cannot. Hence, opener's 4♦ call should be a real cuebid (showing a diamond control), while 4♠ would deny a diamond control and show two top spade honors. Indeed, 4♠ might be passed.

Now try this one:

WEST	EAST
1♡	2♣
3♣	3♦
3NT	4♦
?	

Responder's 4♦ call confirmed 3♦ as a cuebid and converted opener's 3NT call to a non-serious spade-feature bid. Although 4♠ is the unbid major, this auction does not override the general rule that 4♡ is the RKCB bid. Therefore, 4♡ is still RKCB.

Restated: we want 4♡ to be the RKCB call, as it leaves us the most room for answers. A 4♠ bid is only RKCB when hearts offers a known, legitimately viable fit. In this auction, responder cannot want to play 4♡ after inviting 3NT and having been accepted. Thus, hearts have been ruled out. Had opener bid 4♣ instead of 3NT, then 4♡ might still be the right contract. In that case, 4♠ would be RKCB for clubs.

Consequently, in the actual auction, 4♦ has Last Train implications. Opener failed to cuebid 4♣; thus, he lacks good trumps. Therefore, 4♦ is a slam try with poor trumps.

WEST	EAST
1♠	2♣
3♣	3♦
3♡	

This has become an interesting auction. If opener wanted to play 3NT, he would have bid 3NT. Some would play that 3♡ shows a 'bolster', a partial stopper. I prefer to use 3♡ as a cuebid, showing a heart control and serious slam interest. With the bolster, I gamble and bid 3NT anyway — on a good day, partner has the other half-stopper or the suit blocks.

Here we have a new concept. When opener responded to the either-or 3◇ call with 3♡, clearly a cuebid, the rules changed. When one partner makes a try for 3NT and the only way to accept it is to bid 3NT, any other call is a serious slam try and a cuebid.

Once this occurs, 3NT is no longer a possible final contract (although the partnership may stop at 4NT). Instead, 3NT is often equivalent to the 2NT call in major-suit cuebidding, namely showing poor trumps. One could look at it as being similar to a 'Non-Serious 3NT', in that you are 'not serious' only when your trumps are poor.

Now, when I say 'not a possible final contract', I do not mean that the partnership cannot play 3NT. What I mean is that you cannot bid 3NT after a serious cuebid just to claim lack of interest in a slam and express a desire to play 3NT. Instead, 3NT has become an artificial bid, a cuebid denying good trumps (no two of the top three honors). Partner is allowed to use common sense after this bid.

For example, suppose you are dealt:

♠ A K Q 9 6   ♡ A K Q   ◇ —   ♣ J 9 5 4 2

After 1♠-2♣, you would raise clubs. If partner then bid 3◇, you would likely bid 3♡. If partner were to bid 3NT next, denying good trumps, passing would seem like a great idea.

WEST	EAST
1♠	2♣
3♣	3◇
3♡	?

Back to our example auction. Bidding 3NT has been defined as showing poor trumps whenever a minor has been agreed. Cuebidding has evolved from possibly exploring for notrump to clearly exploring for slam. So consider responder's options after opener bids 3♡. He could bid 3♠, showing one of the top three honors in spades. He could bid 3NT, denying a top honor in spades and denying good trumps (which might also induce a reasoned pass). He could bid 4♣, denying a useful spade card and promising good trumps. Hearts is the out-of-focus major and therefore 4♡ is RKCB. Bidding 4◇ would deny a spade honor, promise good trumps and show a diamond control.

You may notice two redundancies here: first, that 4◇ shows a diamond control after a previous 3◇ call. Does this mean that 4◇ is better used as a Last Train call? No. When one person has shown serious slam interest, he is the only one with the right to make a Last Train bid. Thus, in this auction, responder cannot make a Last Train bid. Responder's 4◇ is therefore a cuebid. However, as 3◇ was his prior call, 4◇ should clarify that the diamond control is a 'slam' control. Remember, 3◇ could have been bid with Q-J-10-x, a good 'notrump' feature.

The second redundancy is the 4♣ call. Bypassing 3NT shows two of the top three honors in clubs. Bidding 4♣, a bid below game in the agreed suit, also shows two of the top three honors in clubs. You could, of course, play 4♣ as showing all three top honors in clubs, but there is a more useful way to go.

In a cuebidding sequence with an agreed minor, when 3NT denies good trumps, a bid of four of the agreed minor should show good trumps, but deny the ability to make a cuebid in any other suit below the RKCB call. Thus, if clubs are trumps, 4♣ denies the ability to make a 4◇ cuebid. If diamonds are trumps, bypassing 3NT to bid 4◇ shows good trumps, but denies the ability to make a 4♣ cuebid. No extra message about the agreed suit is exchanged, as this call is an informative waiting bid.

Suppose, then, after opener's 3♡ call, that responder's call was 4♣, showing good trumps, denying the ability to cuebid 4◇ and waiting. Opener could now bid 4♡ as RKCB, but he also has a 4◇ call available. Since he was the one to show serious slam interest, he has the right to bid 4◇ as Last Train. What could he be seeking?

Responder is known to have good trumps, no diamond 'slam' control and no top spade honor. Responder is also known to have diamond values, apparently Q-J-10-x or so. Perhaps opener has really lousy trumps or perhaps opener needs a heart card.

Responder, with something useful, could now bid 4♡ as RKCB.

Otherwise, he could sign off in 4NT or 5♣ or even suggest 4♠ with, perhaps, J-x. Note that a rebid of opener's major after a Last Train bid is not a new cuebid; rather, it declines the Last Train invitation and suggests an alternative strain.

WEST	EAST
1♠	2♣
3♣	3◇
4♣	

Here, opener has declined 3NT, having insufficient heart values. He has also denied serious slam interest, with which he would have cuebid or even bid 4♡, the out-of-focus major, as RKCB for clubs.

Responder may choose to bid 4♡ as RKCB for clubs, confirming his own serious slam interest. He could also bid 4◇ as Last Train, contextually suggesting the need for shortness in hearts in opener's hand (a control which is not a 'notrump' control). Responder might even bid 4♠ to suggest an alternative game. Bidding 4NT would be odd, but I would interpret this as an extended version of the 'weak trumps' cuebid, seeking short hearts, with 4◇ showing good trumps.

Another possible action for opener over the 3◇ 'game try' is simply to jump to 5♣. However, there are two reasons opener should not jump to 5♣ with no heart stopper and a weak hand. First, perhaps responder might have wanted to suggest 4♠ as a viable contract. Second, and more importantly, responder is semi-captain already and may want to continue exploring slam, notwithstanding the lack of a heart card from opener.

What, then, should a jump to 5♣ show? Let's reason it out. Bidding 4NT is a Picture Jump, denying a heart stopper. Bidding 4♠ or 4♡ should also be a Picture Jump. I expect 4♠ to show great spades, no red card and two top club honors. A jump to 4♡ would show great spades, two top club honors and a singleton in hearts. Therefore, 5♣ should show the most important of the missing Picture Jumps, equivalent to the 'Jump to 3NT' option from major-suit cuebidding. It should show two of the top three clubs, two of the top three in the 'second suit' bid by responder (diamonds in the example), insufficient hearts for 3NT, no heart control and no control in spades (opener's suit).

THE PICTURE BID IN THE SIMPLE RAISE SITUATION

If opener starts with a major and hears a minor response, he has the ability to make two types of Picture Jump. He can make a Picture Jump Cuebid to the four-level *in the minor*, which shows good trumps, three of the top four honors in his opened suit and no side control. Opener can also make a Picture Splinter.

Thus,

WEST	**EAST**
1♠	2♣
4♣	

is a Picture Jump Cuebid, while

WEST	**EAST**
1♠	2♣
3♦	

is a Picture Splinter.

Since the preferred strain in the end might be any one of notrump, opener's major or the agreed minor, no Yummy Toes asking bids are used. Instead, the out-of-focus major is simple RKCB.

A few rules must be discussed.

First, opener should be careful not to bypass 3NT to make a Picture Jump in support of a minor unless he has strong slam interest and five-card support for the minor. This rule is necessary to avoid the embarrassment of leaping above 3NT (possibly the best contract). You also have to be careful not to jam partner, who may be intending to show support for your major.

Second, after such a Picture Jump, 4NT establishes the *opened major* as trumps and is RKCB for that major. Remember: responder may have a slam-going hand for opener's major and may just have been bidding his minor to show a source of tricks.

Third, responder may retreat to game in opener's original major, which is to play. A few examples follow.

♠ A Q J 5 3   ♡ 5   ◇ K Q 9 4   ♣ 8 7 6

WEST	EAST
1♠	2◇
3♡	?

Opener starts 1♠ and partner responds 2◇. Jumping to 3♡ now serves a dual purpose. First, it establishes a diamond fit while showing a singleton in hearts, great spades (three of top four honors) and no club control. Since 3NT is not bypassed, it is acceptable to make the bid on a minimum hand.

However, this call also enables responder, on as little as the singleton king of spades, to consider a pseudo-fit in spades as a place to play, usually at matchpoints. Give responder, for example:

♠ K   ♡ A 7 4 2   ◇ A 8 5 3 2   ♣ K Q J

Now 6♠ might be ideal, needing only a 4-3 spade split. Adding a second spade certainly makes 6♠ very comfortable.

Responder can agree spades as trumps in this auction by bidding 4NT (RKCB). The RKCB for diamonds would be 4♡, the out-of-focus major.

♠ A Q J 9 2   ♡ 8 3 2   ◇ K Q 7 5   ♣ 5

WEST	EAST
1♠	2◇
?	

The auction is the same. However, if opener were now to make a Picture Splinter of 4♣, he would bypass 3NT. That may not be desirable on this hand. Add a fifth diamond and convert the spades to A-K-J-x-x; now 4♣ seems great. With the actual hand, 3◇ is probably sufficient.

♠ A K J 10 5   ♡ Q 3   ◇ A K J 3   ♣ 3 2

WEST	EAST
1♠	2◇
?	

The auction is the same again. With 18 HCP opposite 13+, slam must be very close. Bypassing 3NT to bid 4◇ cannot be a terrible move, especially as a Picture Jump to 4◇ describes the hand perfectly.

After a Direct Raise of Opener's 2◇ Rebid

This occurs in only two auctions:

WEST	EAST
1♡	2♣
2◇	3◇

and

WEST	EAST
1♠	2♣
2◇	3◇

In either auction, there are two problems. First, opener may have bid 2◇ on 6-4 pattern. If so, he may be intending to repeat his major later as a natural call. This bid creates an ambiguity, obviously, which should be discussed.

Second, opener may be interested in suggesting 3NT as a contract. To invite 3NT, however, he must be able to bid the fourth suit as an asking bid, not a telling bid. This creates a strange inconsistency. Initially, responder should expect opener to lack values in the unbid major if he bids it. Later, if opener keeps bidding, the three-level bid of the major does not retroactively promise a control, since this would be a problem if responder also has independent, serious slam interest himself. If that occurs, and responder accordingly starts cuebidding, responder should assume that opener lacks values in the other major.

Let's look at an example auction.

WEST	EAST
1♠	2♣
2◇	3◇
?	

If opener is interested in 3NT, but lacks a heart stopper, he can bid 3♡. The bid of the fourth suit, as the only remaining suit, asks rather than tells.

What happens if opener continues cuebidding after responder declines to play in 3NT? Suppose, for example, responder bids 3♠. If opener next bids 4♣, it will show serious slam interest, a club card (queen or higher) and lack of a heart control. Bidding 4♣ directly over 3◇, therefore, would show a club card and also promise a heart control (honor or shortness), with serious slam interest.

Incidentally, this sequence brings up another principle. If opener seems to be trying for 3NT after his diamond suit is raised, responder can bid 3♠ to decline 3NT and show a doubleton spade card. This operates as an either-or bid, as well: either a cuebid for slam purposes or a delayed raise — the remaining auction should clarify which one. This enables the partnership to play a 4♠ contract, if desired.

WEST	EAST
1♠	2♣
2◇	3◇
3♡	3♠
?	

If opener next bids 3NT, it should be viewed as semi-slammish, without a heart control. This is somewhat like a Non-Serious 3NT. The denial cuebid of 3♡ does not change its meaning later. The message is that responder might push toward slam with a shortness-based control in hearts, which is a 'slam' control, but not a 'notrump' control.

Why would opener bid 3NT, though? Any other cuebid, perhaps 4♣, would also reaffirm the lack of a heart control for slam. Bidding 3NT would suggest holding slow values in hearts (Q-x-x perhaps), with slam interest, but such a holding is not a slam control. Opener must have some slam aspirations, but the necessary help in hearts for a slam — shortness — will erase the value of his honor. In any event, 3NT is passable, if one is willing to play 3NT with only one stopper, perhaps because the rest of the hand is so strong. Note that, perforce, opener must have a singleton in clubs for this auction to make sense; also a negative slam feature potentially.

This last point may seem to conflict with the prior discussion of a 'Non-Serious 3NT' as showing poor trumps. Note that the 'Non-Serious 3NT' is not a convention in these circumstances. Rather, it is a tool of thought. When 3NT is bid in a context described as a 'Non-Serious 3NT', the call is meant as natural. However, if partner has slam aspiration, he should *view* the call as meeting certain logical parameters best described as 'non-serious' with specific 'rules', those rules being not so much agreed as inferred.

In the prior context, the 'Non-Serious 3NT' call would have been made by one partner who had suggested 3NT with a cuebid and heard instead a further cuebid from partner in the fourth suit. In that context, bidding 3NT suggested playing there because the trump contribution was poor.

In the context of a *denial cuebid*, interpreted initially as a probe for 3NT and asking for help, 3NT is still natural. The logical inference is that this partner has a 'scary' stopper to offer, like Q-x-x. Offering 3NT in that context suggests great overall strength. Hence, the logic of this different situation suggests that his partner treat his 3NT call differently when assessing slam prospects. As a result, the definition of the inferred 'Non-Serious 3NT' is changed.

In any event, this denial cuebid might be avoided. As always, some Picture Jumps are possible. Responder could have raised diamonds by jumping to 4♡ or 4♣ or opener could advance 3◇ to 4♡ or 4♠, either partner making a Picture Splinter or Picture Jump Cuebid respectively. As is usually the case, however, one should have extra strength to Picture Jump above 3NT when the primary fit is in a minor.

The Preference Establishing a Minor Fit

If responder's 2/1 GF call was 2◇ and his next call was 3♣, he has shown a minor two-suiter. Opener may accept diamonds by bidding 3◇. Now the auction parallels an auction where 2◇ was raised by opener to 3◇, except that Picture Jumps are not available (and those inferences are lost accordingly).

Usually, opener must set clubs by raising to 4♣ if he has bid both majors. However, if opener has rebid his major, a bid of the unbid major should be taken as a probe for 3NT, unless opener cuebids above 3NT; in that case, the previous bid of an unbid major should be taken as a values-denying cuebid. Again, this is a denial cuebid for slam purposes and should be interpreted according to the rules previously described.

If opener's first rebid was 2NT, then his subsequent bid of a new major is artificial and shows club support. The reason for this exception is that opener has already shown notrump tolerance by bidding 2NT, so now a bid of the new major is no longer used to look for 3NT. Three examples:

WEST	EAST
1♠	2♦
2♡	3♣
?	

If opener wants to set diamonds as trumps, he bids 3◇. To set clubs as trumps, opener must bid 4♣, as either 3♡ or 3♠ may be needed as natural. No denial cuebid principles are in effect, as opener has ostensibly shown values in both majors.

WEST	EAST
1♠	2♦
2♠	3♣
?	

Here opener may set diamonds as trumps by bidding 3◇. To set clubs as trumps, opener may raise to 4♣ or bid 3♡. The 3♡ call will be taken, initially, as a probe for a stopper in hearts for 3NT, a values-asking bid. If opener later confirms slam interest, 3♡ will be understood as a denial cuebid. Thus, a 4♣ raise here, inferentially, would show a heart control (honor or shortness). As for the parallel denial cuebid auctions, if responder bids 3♠, opener can bid 3NT to show the queen of hearts, a notrump control and mild slam interest.

WEST	EAST
1♠	2♦
2NT	3♣
?	

Opener, again, can set diamonds as trumps by bidding 3◇. Since notrump has already been introduced, opener can agree clubs with an artificial bid of 3♡, the new major, which says nothing about hearts. Bidding 4♣ instead would be a Picture 'Jump', showing two top club honors and great spades, with no side control. Inferentially, opener *must* have heart 'control' to bid 2NT, but that control must logically be third-round control (Q-J-x, for example).

Remember, here, that 3♡ is like a Flag Bid. It shows a club fit and slam interest, while staying below 3NT. Any other cuebids afterwards would follow ordinary rules.

THE DELAYED RAISE OF RESPONDER'S MINOR

A minor may also be raised at the three-level as a delayed raise. This occurs when responder bids a minor at the two-level, opener bids again at the two-level, responder bids again at the two-level and opener returns to responder's minor (or vice-versa). A few examples:

WEST	EAST
1♠	2♣
2♡	2NT
3♣	

WEST	EAST
1♠	2♣
2♠	2NT
3♣	

WEST	EAST
1♠	2♣
2♦	2♡
3♣	

WEST	EAST
1♠	2♣
2♦	2♡
2NT	3♦

In any of these auctions, we expect three-card support with two top honors. Four-card support is possible if the minor-suit raise was delayed in order to rebid or introduce a major. These auctions should parallel direct-raise auctions, for the most part. However, context tells a lot. Context also defines Picture Jumps.

If, for example, the prior auction made a side singleton mandatory, the Picture Splinter into that suit should show a void — unexpected shortness. A Picture Jump Cuebid would imply no better than a singleton in an already-known short suit.

Some examples. Opener starts the auction with 1♠, holding:

♠ A K 7 5 4 2   ♡ 2   ◇ K Q 10 6   ♣ 4 2

He hears 2◇, which interests him. However, if he immediately raises diamonds, spades may be lost, despite a possible 6-2 fit. So he rebids 2♠.

WEST	EAST
1♠	2◇
2♠	?

Responder continues by bidding 2NT. This allows opener to raise diamonds belatedly, with 3◇, and now his pattern is more or less known.

Suppose opener has:

♠ A K 10 9 3   ♡ K Q 3 2   ◇ K Q 8   ♣ 9

Now, after a 2◇ response to 1♠, opener might rebid 2♡ in the hope of finding a 4-4 heart fit.

WEST	EAST
1♠	2◇
2♡	?

If responder now bids 2NT, opener can bid 3◇ to establish diamonds as trumps. Responder will know, inferentially, that opener has three good diamonds and a singleton club, as 5-4-3-1 pattern is required.

If opener holds, instead

♠ A K 10 9 3   ♡ K Q 3 2   ◇ K Q 8 2   ♣ —

he might still bid 2♡ after 1♠-2◇, hoping to find a 4-4 major fit (or save space if responder next bids 2♠).

WEST	EAST
1♠	2◇
2♡	?

If responder bids 2NT over 2♡, opener can jump to 4♣. This shows a void, as context would imply a mere singleton if opener simply raised diamonds.

A Minor Fit Agreed at the Four-Level

A minor fit can be agreed at the four-level. Instances include when opener high-reverses to a minor, when responder rebids his own minor and when responder introduces a minor as a second suit at the three-level.

WEST	EAST
1♠	2♡
3♣	

WEST	EAST
1♠	2♣
2♢	3♣

WEST	EAST
1♠	2♡
2NT	3♣

These auctions are the most difficult, largely because of the limited space that remains below 3NT. A simple raise of the minor, above 3NT, should show serious slam interest, of course.

When opener's first rebid is 2NT, the introduction of a new minor or the rebid of a minor by responder does allow for better methods. My preference is for any call of a new suit, or a rebid of opener's major, to be a cuebid agreeing the minor and showing at least mild slam interest. Some will be concerned that opener may open a great five-card major (perhaps ♠A-Q-J-10-8), rebid 2NT and then want to rebid his major to show a great suit, albeit only five in length. Personally, I prefer to have this call available as a cuebid.

However, if you want to retain the delayed rebid of opener's suit after 2NT as natural, then only a cuebid of a new suit should agree the minor and show at least mild slam interest. Even with that agreement, if the rebid of opener's major is the only way to show slam interest below 3NT, the natural meaning must be forfeited.

In either event, no specific message is tied to the strain if only one cuebid was available. To clarify, here are a few examples:

WEST	EAST
1♡	2♣
2NT	3♣
?	

If opener now bids 3◇ or 3♠ (or 3♡ if that is the agreement), it is a cuebid in support of clubs. A bid of 3NT by either partner would suggest a signoff; continuing past 3NT would show serious slam interest.

WEST	EAST
1♡	2◇
2NT	3◇
?	

Opener can cuebid 3♠ (or 3♡ if so agreed) to show at least mild interest in a slam in diamonds. Bidding 4♣ instead would show serious slam interest and a first- or second-round control in clubs. If responder does not continue past 3NT, but opener does, then we know that 3♠ was based on serious slam interest, in which case we know that opener has a spade control, even if 3♡ would have been natural. Remember, though, that if opener has only mild slam interest, and a 3♡ bid would have been natural, he might not have a spade control. As the only available cuebid below 3NT, 3♠ would be a sort of 'Last Train' general cuebid below the first best stopping place of 3NT.

WEST	EAST
1♠	2♡
2NT	3♣

Here, 3◇ shows clubs support and slam interest (at least mild). If 3♠ would be natural, 3◇ carries no message about diamonds.

WEST	EAST
1♠	2♡
2NT	3◇

When no cuebid is available to 'raise' the new minor, a rebid of opener's major shows minor support. Here, even if 3♠ would normally be retained as natural, opener can bid 3♠ to agree diamonds.

- 6 -

CUEBIDDING AFTER
UNUSUAL RAISES

Using Modified Bergen 3♣ to Find Slams

In my circle of partners, we use a special version of Bergen Raises that works wonders. We have decided that 3♣ shows any hand with either limit-raise values or a four-card raise with 12-14 HCP and a singleton.

After 1M-pass-3♣, opener typically relays to 3◇ to enable responder to complete his picture, as follows:

3M	=	Minimum limit raise
3OM	=	Splinter (12-14 HCP)
3NT	=	Control rich (four or more controls) max. limit
4M	=	Control poor (fewer than three controls) max. limit
4min	=	5422, tricks source, max. limit
4♡	=	5422, tricks source, max. limit (if spades agreed)

Showing Splinters via 3♣

There are several reasons for showing splinters via our conventional 3♣ call. First, we do not disclose the location of the shortness, and sometimes not even the existence of shortness, when that fact will not benefit us, but may benefit the opponents. Second, it allows the double jumps normally used as splinters to have a different meaning, whether void-showing (my preference) or some other range, like a 15-16 HCP Maxi-splinter. Third, on occasion, opener may want to initiate a cuebidding sequence rather than find out about your shortness; this auction allows cuebidding to start at a lower level.

In any event, 3♣ initiates all 12-14 HCP splinter auctions. If opener is interested in your holding, he will bid 3◇, after which your call of three of the other major will convey that you have shortness, a splinter. After 3OM (three of the other major), opener's cheapest call asks for the singleton. If hearts are trumps, 3OM is 3♠, so 3NT asks. You just bid your singleton, or bid 4♡ with a singleton spade. If spades are trumps, 3OM is 3♡, with 3♠ asking; again, bid the minor singleton or 3NT to show a singleton heart. With spades agreed, there is more room is available for cuebids and Last Train calls.

For example, suppose you hold:

♠ A K 6 3 2   ♡ K Q J   ◇ 9 8 7   ♣ A 3

You open 1♠ and partner leaps to 3♣. In case partner holds the right hand, you ask for more information with 3◇. Partner bids 3♡, the other major, to show a singleton and game-forcing values. Hoping for a singleton diamond, you bid 3♠, the relay, and partner bids 3NT, showing a singleton heart. At this point, passing seems best. However, had partner shown a diamond singleton by bidding 4◇, you would find a nice slam. The full auction would be:

WEST	EAST
1♠	3♣
3◇[1]	3♡[2]
3♠[3]	4◇[4]
6♠	

1. Asking for clarification.
2. GF, Splinter with undisclosed singleton.
3. What singleton?
4. Singleton diamond.

MINIMUM LIMIT RAISE

After a '3M' (three of the agreed major) response to the 3◇ inquiry, cuebids follow traditional rules, with 3NT played as Serious 3NT.

This bid of '3M' is passable, of course, but opener might still have slam interest. Continuing past 3M with a cuebid is slammish, with 3NT being Serious 3NT, not to play. A raise to 4M is a signoff. Although a nine-card major fit might exist in a deal best-suited for 3NT rather than four of the major, such an occasion is rare.

SERIOUS 3NT ANSWER WITH A MAXIMUM LIMIT RAISE

The 'control rich' 3NT is, in a sense, a Serious 3NT response to the 3◇ asking bid. It shows at least two aces or two kings and an ace or possibly four kings (flat). You must also have the values for a 'maximum' limit raise (11-12 HCP). The 'control poor' 4M response shows a maximum limit raise, but denies good controls. (The partnership might agree to treat the trump queen as a 'control' for this purpose, which I advise.)

Consider how this might pay off. Suppose opener starts with 1♡, holding:

♠ K Q 7 6   ♡ K Q J 9 8 4   ◇ K 4   ♣ A

After 3♣, opener fears a death hand opposite something like:

♠ 5 4 3   ♡ A 10 7 5   ◇ Q J 3 2   ♣ K Q

With that hand, however, responder would accept the invite of 3◇ by bidding 4♡, showing poor controls. If we give responder a different hand

♠ J 3 2   ♡ A 7 5 2   ◇ A 7 5 3   ♣ Q J

then getting to slam is easy after he shows good controls via 3NT.

After this 3NT call, opener can use 4♣ to ask for the location of the controls. This parallels the auction after a Serious 3NT in the auction 1M-2M; new suit.

Whenever responder holds two aces, he might still have a king or even the trump queen. If he has two side aces plus the trump king or queen, he should jump to six of the major. With a side king, responder jumps to five of the side king, with 5♡ showing the side king of spades. With only two aces, responder signs off in game. This is the weakest cover-card holding with four controls.

With two kings and an ace, responder should cuebid his lowest card. For example, 4♢ would be a cuebid with two kings and an ace, one of the controls being in diamonds. Four of the other major would deny a diamond king or ace, but show that responder has a king or ace in the other major. A response of 4NT would deny the diamond king or ace and deny the king or ace in the other major; it would show the king or ace of clubs, in a hand with either the other top honor in clubs and a top trump honor or two top trump honors. Opener can keep relaying (bidding the next-up non-trump suit) to ask for additional features, although 4NT is always RKCB. If responder happens to have two kings and an ace and the trump queen, he will decline a signoff by cuebidding another feature, if forced.

If responder holds four kings, we assume that opener could probably figure that out. However, it may be important to show them with a response of 5NT if opener holds something like:

♠ A Q 5 4 3 2   ♡ A Q 4 2   ♢ —   ♣ A Q 8.

From opener's viewpoint, responder might hold four kings or he might hold the diamond ace and any two kings. Four kings are going to be much more useful in a grand slam.

NEW-SUIT BIDS

New-suit bids are akin to Picture Jumps. For example, over an opening bid of 1♠, on a hand like

♠ K 7 5 3   ♡ 5 2   ♢ A Q J 4 2   ♣ 9 7

you might bid 3♣ and then respond to 3◇ with 4◇. This will show one of the top three honors in trumps and a semi-solid second suit, no side control. Yummy Toes asking bids might be used after this, if you like.

Consider how useful this is. With something like the example hand, what would you bid after a 1♠ opening? Bidding 2◇ as a game-forcing start is a tad rich and even more difficult to clarify later. A later Picture Jump after a game-forcing 2◇ would require two top spades, a feature you lack. So, instead, you could try a forcing 1NT, but you'll never be able to describe your hand after that start. Better to try 3♣ and then cuebid 4◇, a 'Picture Jump' without the jump, after the 3◇ asking bid.

Give partner

♠ A 10 9 8 6 2   ♡ 7   ◇ K 8 6   ♣ A 8 3

and an amazingly light but quite decent slam is easily reached.

CUEBIDDING WITHOUT THE 3◇ RELAY

Sometimes opener simply resorts to normal cuebidding. A deal which exemplifies this occurred at the 2005 Seniors Bowl semifinals, where neither team reached the slam on these cards (rotated for convenience):

WEST	EAST
♠ Q 3	♠ K 10 9 7
♡ A K J 9 8 3	♡ Q 10 7 2
◇ A	◇ Q 4 2
♣ K J 8 3	♣ A 5

Using traditional Bergen Raises, the auction was

WEST	EAST
1♡	3◇
4♡	

making +680 — a less-than-inspired result.

Using 3♣ as our limit raise (plus) changes nothing, because 3◇ by West as an asking bid isn't going to produce the information he needs. A better call by West would be a Serious 3NT directly over 3♣, showing serious slam interest without control of spades.

East cooperates with a 4♣ cuebid, showing control of clubs (ace or a singleton, contextually) and control of spades, likely the ace or king. West can pretty much count twelve tricks, so long as East has at least one black ace. He can find out by bidding 4◇ as Last Train, asking if the controls shown so far are honors .

Why does 4◇ ask this question here? Well, if West were interested in shortness, he would have used 3◇ over 3♣, right? If East has honors and not shortness, he should use RKCB himself.

If East is timid and signs off in 4♡ over 4◇, I suppose West could make one last stab with a 4♠ cuebid, showing the spade queen. This might be the nudge that East needs with king-empty in spades.

The Four-Level Minor Rebid

A jump in opener's minor to the four-level is a raise of responder's major bid. It shows 6-4 pattern, a solid minor, good trump support and no side honor control. A typical hand after 1♣-1♠; 4♣ might be:

♠ A J 9 7   ♡ 6   ◇ 9 7   ♣ A K Q 10 3 2.

You can see that this pattern usually features five losers. The trump contribution should include at least K-x-x-x.

After this rebid by opener, responder is usually interested in trump quality and in the location of opener's shortness. For this reason, the cheapest new suit is an asking bid, asking for the location of the singleton. Opener shows his singleton with step responses:

Step One	Singleton in the other minor (lower ranking)
Step Two	Singleton in the other major (higher ranking)

After this answer, 4NT (or the cheapest suit above 4NT if 4NT is unavailable) is RKCB for the major. Normally, 4NT is available. However, if 4NT is the answer to the singleton-ask, then 5♣ is RKCB for the major. In one rare instance, 5♣ is the answer to the singleton-ask, making 5◇ RKCB for the major. More specifics follow.

Club-Major auction (1♣-1M; 4♣)

Here, 4◊ asks for the singleton. Since both possible answers are below 4NT, a subsequent 4NT is RKCB for the major.

Diamond-Spade auction (1◊-1♠; 4◊)

Here, 4♡ is the singleton-asking relay. If opener has a singleton heart, he will respond 4NT, depriving responder of 4NT as RKCB. Accordingly, responder must then bid 5♣ as RKCB. Responder might avoid this problem by bidding 4NT directly over 4◊, if the location of the singleton is not important.

Diamond-Heart auction (1◊-1♡; 4◊)

Notice that the relay here is 4♠, a very awkward bid. Now 4NT by opener should show a singleton club, making 5♣ by responder RKCB for hearts. With a singleton spade, however, opener would bid 5♣, forcing responder to 5◊ as RKCB for hearts. Accordingly, responder may very well opt for 4NT directly.

FIT-SHOWING JUMPS

By a passed hand, a jump shift is often played as a game try with a fit for opener's suit. One might, for instance, jump to 3♣ after a third-seat 1♠ opening with:

♠ Q 5 4 3   ♡ 8   ◊   10 5 2   ♣ A Q J 7 2

This fit-showing jump, sometimes called a 'Flower Bid', shows decent four-card trump support, a great side suit and shape (a singleton). If the Flower Bid is in a major in response to a minor opening, many players relax the strength requirement for the major (K-J-x-x-x perhaps) as long as the minor honor holding compensates.

Clearly, opener, if slammish, will be interested in locating the singleton and in determining the strength of the trump honors. Additionally, after a minor-to-major Flower Bid, the agreed trump suit may shift from the minor to the major.

CONTINUATIONS AFTER A MAJOR-TO-MINOR FLOWER BID

When the opening is in a major, the Flower Bid sets trumps for all cuebidding purposes. This simplifies matters. Opener can use the cheapest available call, other than three or four of the agreed major (either of which shuts down the auction), as a relay. This asks responder to clarify his position.

If responder has a singleton without a control in the other suit, then he bids his singleton. If responder has a control in the fourth suit, perhaps K-x-x or A-x-x, he bids notrump with a singleton in the other minor or the cheapest level of the agreed major with a singleton in the other major. An example:

WEST	EAST
pass	1♠
3♣	?

Opener can sign off in 3♠ or 4♠. If he wants to ask questions, however, he can use the relay, 3◇ in the example. Responder will show the singleton and the side-control information by bidding as follows:

3♡	=	Singleton in hearts, no diamond control
4◇	=	Singleton in diamonds, no heart control
3NT	=	Singleton in diamonds, plus a heart control
3♠	=	Singleton in hearts, plus a diamond control

CONTINUATIONS AFTER A MINOR-TO-MAJOR FLOWER BID

This gets a little trickier, as opener might want to set either suit as trumps. Fortunately, a simple solution exists: Flag Bids. If opener wants to set the minor as trumps, he can bid the other minor as the singleton-asking bid. If he wants to set the major as trumps, he bids the other major as the singleton-asking bid. The reply structure is the same.

Thus:

WEST	EAST
pass	1♣
2♠	3♢
?	

Here, 3♢ asks about the singleton and sets clubs as trumps. A bid of 3♡ instead would carry the same message, but set spades as trumps.

- 7 -

SELF-SUFFICIENT TRUMPS

There are rare occasions in bridge bidding where everything should be easy. Strangely, these are the deals that all too often cause players great difficulty. Take a hand with a self-sufficient trump suit, for example.

Here's a humorous result I once had with the simplest of hands. As a young, crazed player, I was dealt something like:

♠ A K Q J 7 5 3 2   ♡ —   ◊ 4 2   ♣ A K Q

I fantasized a wild auction where I opened 2♣ and had a six-level decision to make at my next call. Ever the innovative one, I opted for a 1◊ opening, figuring that this call was as good as any other. I played 1◊ well for down one. Surprisingly, this was an average, as the field was in 6♠, down one.

These deals now amaze me. Although one partner has a clear direction, the partnership seems unwilling to let him have control. This happens even before the auction introduces a set of questions needing answers.

In actual fact, there are many auctions that allow someone to take control early on. The simplest example is a 2♣ opening, followed by a jump shift. For example:

WEST	EAST
2♣	2◊
3♠	?

Ask the average player and he will have no idea why you jumped. Holding a void in your suit, he will panic and bid strangely. Opener, who executed the jump shift, if he knows what it means, probably has one certainty: that his partner will bid relatively randomly next.

The simple reality is that a bid like this, typically a jump in a shown suit or in the first natural suit in a game-forcing auction, demands that partner give up all pride, accept this suit as trumps, even with a void in it, and cuebid. This is an invaluable and often overlooked agreement.

The following examples demonstrate this technique.

OPENER JUMP REBIDS IN HIS OWN MAJOR IN A 2/1 GF AUCTION

If opener starts 1♠, hears 2♣ as a game-forcing response and leaps to 3♠, this sets spades as trumps and demands cuebidding. Cuebidding follows general rules, including a Serious 3NT option.

Similarly, if 2♣ is a game-forcing response to a 1◊ opening, 3◊ by opener should show a self-playing suit, set trumps and demand cuebidding.

OPENER JUMPS IN A SUIT AFTER 2♣-2◊ (GF)

If opener starts 2♣, hears 2◊ as a Game-Forcing artificial response and jumps to 3♡, this sets hearts as trumps and demands cuebidding. Again, general rules apply, with a Serious 3NT option.

Let's talk a little more about the Serious 3NT call by responder in these auctions. With opener advertising extreme strength, responder can be 'serious' with relatively weak values. Remember that an unbalanced 2♣ opening is often described as showing at least 8½ tricks. Assuming this strength, responder needs only about three tricks to have a 50-50 slam prospect.

However, the Serious 3NT call is usually intended to grab captaincy, which makes little sense in an auction starting with 2♣. Opener is almost always in a superior position to assess the value of specific honors, as opposed to trying to describe his entire hand for responder. Accordingly, the Serious 3NT option should be specifically defined. How you define it will, to some extent, depend on your requirements for opener's jump in his own suit. Personally, I prefer to play that the jump rebid does not promise a solid suit. For example, with a suit like ♠A-K-J-9-7-4-3, I feel comfortable demanding that my suit be trumps. This is not standard. Most play that a jump rebid by a 2♣ opener shows a solid suit, and the same requirement applies to a jump rebid of a major after a 2/1 GF call. If you hold fast to this requirement, then the meaning of 'serious' changes accordingly. I suggest that the 3NT call by responder in this sort of auction shows at least two keycards (or one keycard and the trump queen), plus a singleton and good trump support.

For example:

WEST	EAST
2♣	2◇
3♠	?

With

♠ Q 8 6   ♡ 6   ◇ A 10 4 3 2   ♣ 8 6 5 4

you have serious slam interest. Bid 3NT. With the lesser

♠ Q 8 6   ♡ 6 4   ◇ A 10 4 3 2   ♣ 8 6 5

simply bid 4◇, denying a singleton if a second keycard is held.

If opener hears the Serious 3NT call, he can bid 4♣, an artificial call asking responder to bid his singleton. Responder will bid his singleton if it is in diamonds (4◇), hearts (4♡) or spades (4♠). If responder's singleton is in clubs, he bids four of the agreed trump suit. With three or more keycards and no singleton, responder pretends that opener bid 4NT as RKCB and gives the agreed five-level response.

After the response to 4♣ describing the singleton, cuebidding can continue or opener may use RKCB.

OPENER JUMPS IN A SUIT AFTER 2♣-2♡ (NEGATIVE)

Many people misunderstand the 2♡ negative response to a 2♣ opening. The act of making a negative response to 2♣ does not relieve partner of the obligation to make another call. Thus, a rebid of 2♠ by opener would still be forcing. Similarly, 3♠, a jump, would still set trumps and demand cuebidding, albeit in a much more limited circumstance, offering responder fewer options.

Here, again, a Serious 3NT by responder is possible. Consider the limitations on this, however. If 2♡ denied an ace or king or two queens, then logically a hand is only 'serious' if one holds the trump queen, a side singleton and trump length. Accordingly, after

WEST	EAST
2♣	2♡
3♠	

I would expect 3NT to show something like:

♠ Q 6 2   ♡ 9 7 4 3   ◇ 7   ♣ 8 5 4 3 2

Now, 4♣ by opener would, as before, ask for the singleton.

These auctions are also specific as to the bidding of controls. Responder may cuebid queens or singletons (with trump support). For example, after 2♣-2♡; 3♠, responder might cuebid 4♣ to show either a singleton club and trump length (without the trump queen) or the club queen.

Once a cuebid like this is made, it is not possible for responder's hand to include any other feature, except perhaps a stray jack. What opener may want to know, however, is what responder's cuebid shows precisely. Opener may use a series of relays to ask specific questions.

Here's an example:

WEST	EAST
2♣	2♡
3♠	4♣
?	

Responder has shown that he has either the club queen or a singleton with length in trumps. Opener can seek clarification via the relay (the next bid up) of 4◇. Responder clarifies his holding as follows:

Step One (4♡)	=	the queen
Step Two (4♠)	=	a singleton, trump length
Step Three (4NT)	=	a void, trump length

After a Step One response (here, 4♡), opener can bid the next relay (skipping trumps, so not 4♠) to ask for more information. If responder has any other feature, now is the time to show it. A feature would include any stray jack or a doubleton with good trumps (3+). To show a feature in the relay suit, responder can bid notrump, if possible. Responder should not, however, bypass the next level of our trump suit to show a feature.

After a Step Two or Step Three response, a relay from opener asks about trump length, in steps. The first step shows three trumps; each step above that shows an additional trump card. This tells opener how many tricks he can expect from the shortness. After this question is answered, opener can make yet another relay to ask for any stray jacks.

Setting Trumps as Responder to a 1NT Opening

In several instances, responder can set trumps after a 1NT opening. Often, he can show pattern also.

After a Jacoby Transfer

Suppose the auction begins:

WEST	EAST
1NT	2◇
2♡	?

If responder jumps to 3♠, 4♣ or 4◇, he shows in each case a singleton or void, sets hearts as trumps and encourages cuebidding. A simple jump to 4♡, in contrast, is akin to a Last Train bid, because responder did not use Texas. Hence, responder has mild slam interest.

AFTER STAYMAN

The same principle applies, to a degree, after a major-suit response to Stayman: a bid of three of the other major sets opener's major as trumps and demands cuebidding. A splinter might also be used.

Consider an auction.

WEST	EAST
1NT	2♣
2♠	3♡
?	

Responder has set spades as trumps. Opener might now cuebid 3♠ (good trumps), 3NT (Serious, but poor trumps, because he bypassed 3♠) or a new suit (non-serious, with poor trumps).

SELF-SPLINTERING

If one partner bids notrump as an opening or response and shows no other suit, his partner may set trumps by showing one suit and then making an unnecessary splinter jump into another suit. This, as always, sets the first suit as trumps, shows shortness and demands cuebidding. Serious 3NT and Last Train are used, as appropriate.

Two examples. (1) Partner opens 1NT and you transfer to spades by bidding 2♡. You then jump to 4♣. This sets spades as trumps and shows club shortness. Opener can now cuebid. (2) You open 1♠ and partner bids 1NT, forcing. A jump by you to 4♣ would be a splinter, setting spades as trumps and initiating cuebidding.

- 8 -

COMPLICATED
AUCTIONS

USING CUEBIDDING AFTER TWO-WAY CHECKBACK STAYMAN

As you can probably see, the more complicated the auction leading up to cuebidding, the more complicated the cuebidding. Still, rules are rules.

MAJOR SUIT FOCUS AFTER TWO-WAY CHECKBACK 2◇

Consider a deal I once faced with a good friend and partner. I held:

♠ Q 8 7   ♡ A Q 8 4   ◇ J 10 9 7   ♣ A 5

For the purposes of this discussion, assume I decide on a 1◇ opening. Partner held:

♠ A J 10 9 3   ♡ 9 5   ◇ A Q 6 3 2   ♣ 7

How should these hands be bid to reach the roughly 75% contract of 6◇?

After my 1◇ opening, partner would bid 1♠. I now rebid 1NT, limiting my hand systemically to about 11-13 HCP or a bad 14 HCP (we stretch to open 1NT on 14+ HCP in first or second seat). After 1NT, we have a structure that we like, which includes Two-Way Checkback Stayman. In this structure, we use a direct bid of 3♣ or 3◊ as invitational, 3♣ being canapé (longer clubs than spades). A direct raise to 2NT is actually a relay to 3♣, showing a weak minor canapé. So 2◊ is a general game force and may show any number of hands. For example, it would be a reasonable call with 5-5 pattern, two aces, body and a known fit in diamonds.

The principles I will discuss work the same way for a simplified New Minor Forcing approach, with one simple adjustment, described at the end.

After 2◊, I would, by agreement, bid 2♠, partner's suit, since I have a fragment.

ME	PARTNER
1◊	1♠
1NT	2◊
2♠	?

This sequence does not establish an eight-card spade fit. Partner may well have a spade-minor canapé with game-forcing values. Structurally, however, partner has three options after my 2♠ call: he can establish diamonds as trumps by bidding 3◊; he can raise spades to 3♠ to set spades as trumps; or he can make any call that is logically a cuebid, such as a Picture Jump to 4♠ or a Picture Splinter to 4♣, 4◊ or 4♡. Note that immediate picture bids agree the last-bid suit, as always (spades in this auction).

So what about 2NT from partner? Perhaps, if partner held a relatively balanced hand, 2NT should be slammish and quantitative. Or perhaps 2NT is a 'poor trumps' cuebid agreeing spades. An agreement needs to be reached here. I propose a simple solution after a Game-Forcing 2◊ Checkback when opener rebids in responder's first-bid major:

1. 2NT by responder agrees the major and shows poor trumps;
2. Three of opener's minor sets that minor as trumps;
3. Three of the other minor is natural (and in our case, canapé-style) and game-forcing;
4. 3NT is quantitative;
5. Jumps are Picture Jumps, agreeing the major;
6. The other major is a cuebid, agreeing the major (and showing good trumps).

So in this auction,

WEST	EAST
1♢	1♠
1NT	2♢
2♠	?

responder can bid:

2NT, agreeing spades but showing poor trumps;

3♢, setting diamonds as trumps;

3♣, as natural, showing 4 spades and 5+ clubs;

3NT is quantitative;

4♣, 4♢ and 4♡ are Picture Splinters;

3♡ is a cuebid in support of spades, with good trumps;

3♠, agreeing spades, good trumps, with no heart control.

Back to the example:

ME	PARTNER
♠ Q 8 7	♠ A J 10 9 3
♡ A Q 8 4	♡ 9 5
♢ J 10 9 7	♢ A Q 6 3 2
♣ A 5	♣ 7
1♢	1♠
1NT	2♢
2♠	?

Partner could logically elect to start the cuebidding sequence with spades 'agreed' as trumps. His plan might be to sign off in 4♠ or to plunge into 6♢ if, and when, enough information is obtained. He would, therefore, elect to cuebid 2NT at this stage, setting spades as trumps, but denying two top spade honors.

I, of course, cuebid 3♣ to show a club control. Partner then cuebids 3♢, promising one of the top three diamond honors. I continue 3♡, showing a heart control. Partner now cuebids 3♠, promising one top spade honor. Back to me.

ME	PARTNER
♠ Q 8 7	♠ A J 10 9 3
♡ A Q 8 4	♡ 9 5
◇ J 10 9 7	◇ A Q 6 3 2
♣ A 5	♣ 7

1◇	1♠
1NT	2◇
2♠	2NT
3♣	3◇
3♡	3♠
?	

At this point, I face a situation analogous to the one where, with a limited, balanced hand, I open 1♠ and rebid 2NT, after which partner sets spades as trumps. The rule for that situation is that I am 'serious' about slam if I have six controls, counting the trump queen as a control. This usually means two trump honors and two side aces, or three aces. Thus, a Serious 3NT call by me could show something like:

♠ K Q 8   ♡ A 8 5   ◇ J 10 8 3   ♣ A 8 2

I am a tad shy of this. With no other cuebid to make, I am forced to sign off in 4♠, leaving partner with a tough decision. My 4♠ bid will likely end the slam investigation.

Suppose, however, that instead of bidding 2NT over 2♠ to agree spades, partner set diamonds as trumps by bidding 3◇. I could then cuebid 3♡, showing a heart control. Partner then bypasses 3♠ (denying two top spade honors), bypasses 3NT (non-serious, with poor trumps) and cuebids 4♣, showing a club control, good trumps, only one spade honor and serious slam interest.

ME	PARTNER
♠ Q 8 7	♠ A J 10 9 3
♡ A Q 8 4	♡ 9 5
◇ J 10 9 7	◇ A Q 6 3 2
♣ A 5	♣ 7

1◇	1♠
1NT	2◇
2♠	3◇
3♡	4♣
?	

This interests me, as I have two key aces and a spade card, but not enough to take control of the auction. My heart queen is of questionable value and I lack any secondary cards in our suits, except that spade queen. I temporize with a 4◇ call, which should be taken here as Last Train. I have enough to encourage partner, so I push.

Partner accepts this try and bids 4♡, the out-of-focus major, as RKCB for diamonds. With two keycards, but no diamond queen, I respond 5♣. Partner will expect, at worst, the diamond king and heart ace, but that would not be enough for a Last Train call — I must have a spade card also, or two aces, or something of note. So 6◇ is a fair bet and partner will probably take a shot at it.

The key lessons from this auction are summarized below. When responder bids 2◇ as Game-Forcing Checkback and opener shows three-card support for his major:

1. 2NT is a cuebid showing poor trumps;
2. 3NT is quantitative;
3. Jumps also establish the major as trumps and are Picture Bids;
4. Opener should show serious slam interest and can bid Serious 3NT with two cards in the major and two side aces, or three aces;
5. Opener can rebid four of his minor as Last Train;
6. Responder can set opener's minor as trumps by bidding it next;
7. If opener's minor is set as trumps, 3NT is non-serious.

If NMF is used instead, our auction would have begun:

WEST	EAST
1◇	1♠
1NT	2♣
2♠	?

The same structure applies, except that a raise to 3♠ is invitational.

An example of where this structure could have gained quite a few IMPs came up in the finals of the 2005 Bermuda Bowl on this deal (rotated):

WEST	EAST
♠ A 7	♠ J 10 8 5
♡ 9 6 5	♡ A Q J 10 8 3 2
◇ A 10 8 4 3	◇ —
♣ A 10 7	♣ K Q

West opens 1◊, either nebulous or standard, and receives a response of 1♡. Assuming a style where ♡9-6-5 is insufficient support for a raise (a style that actually hurts this auction), West will rebid 1NT. East, with such a quality heart suit, can certainly justify bidding 2◊, game-forcing, as a precaution. This pays off when opener bids 2♡.

WEST	EAST
1◊	1♡
1NT	2◊
2♡	?

East can visualize a possible slam if opener has three aces, certainly reasonable, so he sets trumps by bidding 3♡. This shows good trumps, because of the failure to cuebid 2NT. Notice that a 2♠ bid by East could not possibly be natural here — it must be a cuebid for hearts. The 3♡ raise therefore also denies a spade control.

Back to West. He has a 'minimum' hand by HCP analysis. However, he couldn't have a much better hand after the simple 1NT rebid. If we add the trump queen, a first-seat 1NT opening probably would have been the option. He has three aces, meaning six controls, and a potentially useful doubleton in spades. He has serious slam interest and should show it by bidding 3NT.

There is another way to view West's problem. If East is slammish, as he must be for his failure to sign off simply in 4♡, his interest is based on a hand with at most one ace, probably the trump ace. Certainly first-round control of all side suits is something that East must be interested in hearing about. When holding great trumps, you should stretch to show 'serious' slam interest. Equally, when you hold an extraordinarily high number of aces, you should stretch. So here, a Serious 3NT will give East grounds to venture further. A bad possible hand from West would be something like:

♠ 7 3 2   ♡ K 5 4   ◊ A Q 5 3 2   ♣ A 7

However, when East failed to cuebid 2♠, he denied a spade control. Hence, West's Serious 3NT call must guarantee a spade control.

Adding the spade king in, one could visualize:

♠ K 3 2   ♡ K 5 4   ◊ A 5 4 3 2   ♣ A 7

However, this hand lacks either three aces or two aces plus two heart honors, so it's definitionally and practically insufficient for the Serious 3NT call.

The 3♡ call from West ruled out the top two heart honors option, so we know for sure that West has three aces. Definitions would have resolved this, but logic sometimes aids memory, right?

You might protest that West cannot have a spade control, since he did not cuebid 3♠. This seems accurate, until you reconsider the auction. Opener must have a spade control to continue cuebidding. With no spade control in either hand, he would simply sign off in 4♡. This brings us to a unique cuebidding principle.

If a player must have a control in the next available suit in order to cuebid, he need not cuebid that suit to show a control in that suit. Any other cuebid will also show a control in that suit. Thus, 3NT by West shows serious slam interest directly and shows spade control inferentially, clearly the ace. Responder should expect something like:

$$♠ A 3 2 \quad ♡ 9 5 4 \quad ◇ A 5 4 3 2 \quad ♣ A 5$$

If the 1◇ opening was standard, responder can be assured of at worst 3-3-4-3 pattern. With a nebulous 1◇, the pattern might be as divergent as 3-3-2-5, but slam has reasonable prospects when the heart finesse works. Opener might have a doubleton spade. If opener has a third spade, only a spade lead seriously frustrates opportunities for simple spade pitches on the minor aces, and that risk only materializes when North has all three outstanding hearts. Counterbalancing this is the chance that opener might have a trick source in clubs, especially if 1◇ was nebulous. For example, opener might have

$$♠ A 3 \quad ♡ 9 5 4 \quad ◇ A 5 4 3 \quad ♣ A J 10 5$$

enabling a third spade pitch. Whether he decides to go on or not, responder certainly has a great deal of information justifying strong consideration of the roughly 50% slam. This information is available to him without committing to the five-level.

MINOR-SUIT AGREEMENT AFTER TWO-WAY CHECKBACK 2◇

The 2◇ game-forcing checkback call can also lead to a slam-going auction with a minor suit as the focus. Normally, this is not a problem when responder bids 2◇ and bids opener's minor to focus it. The problem arises when opener inconveniently shows extra values in his minor suit after 2♦ starts the Forcing Checkback sequence.

Consider this simple example: after 1♦-1♠; 1NT, you, as responder, hold five spades and four diamonds, with slam interest. You bid 2♦, hoping for a 2♠ call. At worst, partner will bid 2♥ or 2NT, which will enable a nice 3♦ call to focus diamonds as trumps. Frustratingly, partner gets in the way with his good news and bids 3♦. Sure, he has 5332 with a maximum and five diamonds — this is good news. But what do you do? Raising to 4♦ gives up a world of cuebids. The auction so far:

WEST	EAST
1♦	1♠
1NT	2♦
3♦	?

After opener rebids his minor, the 'simple' solution is to play that three of the unbid major agrees opener's minor for slam purposes and is a 'general' cuebid, sort of a 'Flag Bid'. This call merely agrees trumps and suggests that cuebidding commence. So, with the problem hand, you would cuebid 3♥ as a Flag for diamonds, agreeing diamonds and asking for cuebids. The 3♥ bid would say nothing about hearts.

CUEBIDDING AFTER 2NT REBIDS

When opener holds about 18 HCP, balanced, there is good news and bad news. The good news is that opener has a very strong hand. The bad news is that he is going to preempt his own auction to show this.

There are some conventions that can help you handle this predicament. If the partnership uses a good treatment, cuebidding should be made somewhat easier. I'm going to describe a few useful gadgets and then discuss cuebidding on the assumption that you play them.

MODIFIED WOLFF SIGNOFF

After a 1min-1M opening and a 2NT Jump Rebid, 3♣ is a semi-relay to 3♦. This is a Wolff Signoff. Opener is supposed to support responder's major with three-card support or bid 3♦ otherwise. For example:

WEST	EAST
1◇	1♡
2NT	?

Responder can now bid 3♣ as a Wolff Signoff. If opener holds three hearts, he bids 3♡; otherwise, he bids 3◇. Responder can then make another suit call as a slam try in opener's minor. In traditional Wolff Signoff, a direct 3◇ over 2NT is Checkback Stayman. All of this means that slam tries in the other minor (the one not opened) become rather difficult.

My preferred treatment is slightly different.

(1) 3◇ is a slam try for opener's minor, whichever one was opened.

Opener can, at this point, cuebid in the normal manner, as if the minor had been raised in a game-forcing auction, with 3NT available as a signoff suggestion (poor trumps). The one difference is that cuebids are automatically deemed cuebids for slam purposes and not ambiguous (possible notrump probes). Picture Jumps (4♡ and 4♠) are possible. The Picture Jump into responder's major shows two top honors in responder's major, two top honors in the opened minor and both side aces, e.g.

WEST	EAST
1◇	1♠
2NT	3◇
4♠	

♠ K Q 9   ♡ A 5 4   ◇ K Q 9 7   ♣ A 4 3 2

The Picture Jump into the other major shows aces in the two side suits, two top honors in the agreed minor and A-x or K-x in responder's major, e.g.

WEST	EAST
1◇	1♠
2NT	3◇
4♡	

♠ K 2   ♡ A 5 4   ◇ A Q 9 8 5   ♣ A J 4

(2) 3♣ is a 'soft' relay to 3♢.

WEST	EAST
1♢	1♠
2NT	3♣

By 'soft', I mean that opener has the option of bidding 3♡ instead of 3♢ in one limited circumstance. If clubs are opened and hearts are the response, then 3♡ shows three hearts and no more than a doubleton in diamonds. In all other sequences, opener must bid 3♢. Technically, this kind of relay (where responder has options) is called a 'marionette' (as opposed to a 'puppet', which forces a specific response).

In most auctions, 3♢ is the response, which can be passed. If responder continues by bidding three of his major, this is to play. If responder bids three of the other major, it is a slam try for the other minor. Opener may decline this by bidding 3NT or he may accept with a cuebid or a simple raise.

Here are some example auctions:

WEST	EAST
1♢	1♠
2NT	3♣
3♢	3♡[1]
3NT[2]	

1. A slam try in clubs.
2. Declined.

WEST	EAST
1♢	1♠
2NT	3♣
3♢	3♠[1]
pass	

1. To play.

(3) *When responder has interest in one or both of the majors, he bids naturally.*
As is usually the case, opener may superaccept a repeated major by cue-bidding. Alternatively, after a new major call, opener may use Flag Bids (4♣ for hearts, 4◇ for spades) to superaccept.

WEST	EAST
1◇	1♠
2NT	3♡¹
4◇²	4♡³
etc.	

1. Natural.
2. Flag agreeing spades.
3. Cuebid for spades.

AFTER 1♣-1◇; 2NT

Focusing a minor is easy. Responder bids 3♣ to establish a club fit and sug-gest normal club-fit cuebidding. Meanwhile, 3◇ suggests diamonds as a fit and invites cuebid acceptances or 3NT rejection. It's a little trickier when responder wants to introduce a four-card major over 2NT.

WEST	EAST
1♣	1◇
2NT	3♡
?	

If the new major is hearts, opener can use 3♠ as a general cuebid to agree hearts, allowing responder room for a Serious 3NT. Alternatively, opener can reject both suits by bidding 3NT, which is semi-forcing by dint of the overall strength of the two hands. Any other call above 3NT agrees dia-monds and is either a cuebid or RKCB (other major), as appropriate, with 4◇ possibly a waiting bid without two top club honors to show.

WEST	EAST
1♣	1◇
2NT	3♠
?	

If the new major is spades, we can simply use 4♣ as an artificial agreement of spades and 4◊ as a natural agreement of diamonds. We can reserve 4♡ for hands with very poor slam interest under the circumstances, but a spade fit.

AFTER 1♡-1♠; 2NT

This is the last possibility. Responder might have continuing slam interest with two main types of hand: two-suiters with five spades or two-suiters with four spades, a longer minor and just less than game-forcing strength. Here is the structure I recommend.

(1) With the former hand type, responder bids 3♣, Checkback. Any call except 3◊ by opener agrees spades and is a cuebid, even 3NT (opener bids 3◊ with any non-fit). On a hand without a spade fit, opener bids 3◊ to enable responder to show a five-card minor with slam interest, if desired. After 3◊, responder can use Flag Bids to show his secondary minor suit: 3♡ for clubs or 3♠ for diamonds. Thus, with 5-5 in the black suits, responder first bids 3♣. If spades are agreed, great! If not, opener will bid 3◊, allowing responder to bid 3♡ for clubs. After this delayed Flag Bid, cuebids are on with the minor agreed, unless opener bids 3NT.

(2) With a longer minor, for example a 4-5 or 4-6 hand, responder may bid 3◊, natural and game-forcing, or cuebid 3♡, an artificial bid showing clubs. Cuebids follow or else 3NT by opener suggests a signoff.

(3) An immediate 3♠ shows long spades and is passable.

This treatment might have helped to avoid a 10-IMP loss in the 2002 Spingold Finals on this deal (hands rotated):

WEST	EAST
♠ A K	♠ 10 7 4 2
♡ A K J 4 3	♡ 10 6
◊ K J 4	◊ A Q 5 3 2
♣ 10 9 2	♣ A 7

The pair who missed slam started like this:

WEST	EAST
1♡	1♠
2NT	?

East, unable to visualize a possible diamond slam, dropped the ball by bidding 3NT, a signoff.

Using the treatment proposed above, East should simply bid 3◇, which shows longer diamonds than spades and slam interest. West loves this and can cuebid 3♡, showing two of the top three hearts. East can now cuebid 4♣, showing good trumps (he did not bid 3NT) and a club control, with poor spades.

WEST	EAST
1♡	1♠
2NT	3◇
3♡	4♣
?	

This is enough for West, who can wield 4♠ as RKCB for diamonds (not 4♡, which might sound like a signoff, lacking spade control).

THE EMPATHETIC SPLINTER

A 1NT opening tightly limits high-card strength and obviously denies shortness. What, then, would a bid that sounds like a splinter really be after a 1NT opening? A doubleton? Possibly, but there is a better use for these calls.

The 'best' hand for opener to invite a slam on would be one that fits well opposite a splinter by responder. Sometimes, however, responder cannot make a splinter, or he might downgrade a singleton because of expected values from opener in that suit or because a fit is not yet known.

To cater to this situation, on rare occasions, you can make a call that shows acceptance of a hypothetical splinter from partner. I call this the 'Empathetic Splinter', because you are imagining a possible hand where partner might have slam interest due to shortness, but is unable to show that interest. You make a call that tells partner that you would have made a move over that splinter.

AFTER STAYMAN

Suppose that you open 1NT with:

♠ A Q 5 3   ♡ 9 7 4 2   ◇ A K 8   ♣ A 5

If partner uses Stayman (2♣), you may very well be systemically required to bid 2♡. Suppose that partner now bids 2♠, which you play as showing an invitational hand with four spades.

WEST	EAST
1NT	2♣
2♡	2♠
?	

Is slam possible? Sure. Partner might have a singleton heart, four spades, five diamonds and a few points, right? For example, he might have:

♠ K 8 7 6   ♡ 5   ◇ Q 9 6 4 2   ♣ K 8 2

With that hand, we can expect to take four spades naturally, at least one heart ruff, five diamonds and two clubs, for twelve tricks. Thus, it might be useful to have a method of showing all the features necessary for a remote slam, namely good trumps, no wasted values in hearts, a great minor fragment and first-round control of the other minor.

Although the circumstance in which it would be used is extremely rare, we define a jump to four of a minor, in this auction, as a Picture Jump, showing good trumps (two of the top three spades), no wasted heart honors (J-x-x-x or worse), a great fragment in the bid minor (K-Q-x or better) and first-round control of the other minor. Any one card can be 'moved': thus, one might have A-K-Q-x in spades, but only A-x-x in the minor fragment. In other words, the Picture Jump here shows five of the seven cover cards, those being the top three spades, the top three cards in the minor fragment and the ace of the other minor. The Picture Jump identifies the minor fragment.

AFTER A JACOBY TRANSFER

In the 2000 Team Olympiad finals between Italy and Poland, the Italians missed a rare opportunity for a second type of Empathetic Splinter on these hands (rotated):

WEST	EAST
♠ 9 7 4 3	♠ 5
♡ Q 5 4	♡ A K J 10 7
◊ A K Q 4	◊ 10 6
♣ A 9	♣ K 8 5 3 2

West opened 1NT and East started to transfer to 2♡ when South intervened over 2◊ by bidding 2♠. West passed this around to East, who doubled. West jumped to 4♡, ending the auction.

Our second type of Empathetic Splinter would have saved the Italians an 11-IMP loss on this deal. West denied tremendous values when he opted not to bid 3♡ directly over 2♠. For good reason, however, he decided that four little spades in his hand probably fit with an anticipated likely shortness in spades from East. This is a perfect recipe for an Empathetic Splinter and it should be part of your arsenal here.

When partner transfers to a major and interference occurs in the other major, opener may employ a bid of four of a minor to show length but no wasted honors in the opposition's major, good trumps, a great fragment in the minor bid and first-round control in the other minor. A delayed bid implies a lesser trump holding with a compensating better minor holding. A similar call could be made after minor-suit interference.

On this deal, West can bid 4◊ over South's 2♠. East will 'see' West's exact hand, just about, and will venture the slam accordingly. At worst, West will have:

$$♠ 6 4 2 \quad ♡ Q 6 4 \quad ◊ A Q J 3 \quad ♣ A Q 9$$

In that case, the slam will be on a diamond finesse.

AFTER A PREEMPTIVE OPENING

An interesting problem was once presented to me while smoking between rounds. (This is, of course, where all great bridge problems are discussed.) You hold

♠ 4 3 2   ♡ A K Q J 10   ◇ A   ♣ K Q 8 7

and partner opens 3♣. What next?

The answers given by fellow smokers were in two batches. One group espoused the art of the game, electing to leap to 6♣ 'to make the opponents guess the right lead'. The other group initially discussed science, but had no idea what science applied in this situation and retreated to art. So, what is the science here?

When partner makes a preemptive opening, it is fair to assume that he has some 7321 pattern, with no side aces or kings. Hence, the most likely 'control' is the singleton. Now, a great little tool can be used.

Over most preempts at the three-level, 4♣ by partner shows serious slam interest and agrees opener's suit as trumps. Opener can now simply cuebid his side control, if he has one. We expect this to be a singleton. Without a side control, opener rebids his suit.

When the preempt is 3♣, responder uses 4◇ as the control-asking bid, with opener's rebid of 4NT showing a diamond control (usually a diamond singleton).

Look at the example hand. After 3♣, the science would be to bid 4◇ to set clubs as trumps and show serious slam interest. On the actual deal, opener would rebid 4♠, presumably a singleton spade. It's easy to bid 6♣ now, but can we do better?

When opener shows a control, responder can ask for more information by 'raising' the cuebid. Thus, after 4♠, responder could bid 5♠ to invite the grand if opener has a void (or the ace) in spades.

Thus, if you like science, the answer to the smoker's quiz is to bid 4◇, setting clubs as trumps, to see if partner can cuebid 4♠. On this deal, the small slam would have been reached and the grand sniffed at.

The same principle and convention can be used effectively after a weak two-bid, followed by Ogust. As a simple example, consider this auction:

WEST	EAST
2♠	2NT
3♢	4♣
?	

Opener has shown bad-hand-good-suit. Now, responder can bid 4♣ to see if opener has a singleton. If opener rebids 4♢, we can expect something like:

$$♠ A Q J 8 7 5 \quad ♡ 9 3 2 \quad ♢ 8 \quad ♣ 9 5 2.$$

You should recognize that this 4♣ call is similar to one we discussed earlier. After a 2♣ opening and a jump rebid by opener, we encountered the 4♣ inquiry after a 'Serious 3NT' bid by the responder. Consistent structure is a good thing.

Here's an example of this 4♣ convention in practice. Remember on this deal that a 4♣ call after a preempt technically asks for cuebids, not specifically for shortness: we just assume, in many sequences, that the control is shortness. That is not necessarily the case. Take an example from the 2005 Vanderbilt Finals where both teams missed a slam. The hands are rotated.

WEST	EAST
♠ A 2	♠ K J 4
♡ J 9 7 6 4 2	♡ A K 10 8 5
♢ K 4	♢ A 10 6
♣ J 10 2	♣ K 5

At both tables, West opened 2♡. This seems wrong to me, but who am I to judge? I never played in the Vanderbilt Finals. I suppose 2♡ is the normal opening in that event.

Anyway, East can start, logically, with 2NT (Ogust) and will hear 3♡, good-hand-bad-suit. The one team to reach at least 5♡ now used RKCB and, finding one ace, resigned in 5♡. This seems odd and futile. Apparently, East was hoping that West held:

$$♠ A 2 \quad ♡ J 9 7 6 4 2 \quad ♢ 4 3 \quad ♣ A 10 2$$

Now try the auction with our conventional 4♣ call after the response to Ogust. As we discussed, this asks opener to cuebid and agrees hearts as trumps. Opener cuebids 4◊, of course. Now, when responder asks for aces, he expects either the actual hand or a hand with a black ace and a diamond singleton. This might be just enough to bid the slam.

On the next deal, the 4♣ call after Ogust would have, unfortunately, put me in a failing slam on a deal from the 2005 Seniors Bowl Playoff in Estoril, had I been participating in the event. These were the hands:

WEST	EAST
♠ K J	♠ A Q 10 9 4 2
♡ A J 9 6 2	♡ 7 3
◊ A 9	◊ 6 5
♣ A Q 9 3	♣ K 8 4

After East opens 2♠, I would venture 2NT Ogust and hear good-hand-good-suit. Wielding 4♣, agreeing spades and asking for a cuebid, I would have elicited 4♠ from East. Contextually, especially given my spade holding, East, with a 'good hand', cannot logically have zero controls in the side suits. Since he bypassed 4◊ and 4♡, he must have a club control.

The worst hand that I could visualize would be:

♠ A Q 10 9 4 2   ♡ 7 4 3   ◊ 6 5   ♣ K 8

The slam makes if the hearts come in for one loser or if I do not get a diamond lead. Opposite the actual hand, I make if the clubs split 3-3 or if restricted choice works when North drops an honor under the king or if I don't get a diamond lead. Therefore, I would bid the slam.

Unfortunately, on the actual deal, a diamond lead from South is obvious and the clubs misbehave. Luck (and judgment) is still part of this game.

CUEBIDDING AS A SUPERACCEPTANCE

If you open 2NT, strong and balanced, partner will often respond by transferring to a major. This auction may result in a missed slam because opener lacks understanding of the implications of this development. All too frequently, people assume that the tight range of 20-21, for example, has told the full tale. This is untrue.

Consider partner's problem after a 2NT opening if he holds a distributional hand like this one:

♠ K 9 6 5 4 2   ♡ 2   ◇ K Q 8 4   ♣ 4 3

Opposite a hand like

♠ A 10 3   ♡ A 9 7 5   ◇ A 9 7 3   ♣ A K

a 'mere' 19-HCP hand, you want to be in 6♠ and might even make seven.

However, what if opener has:

♠ J 3   ♡ K Q J 8   ◇ A J 7 5   ♣ A K Q

Opposite 21 points of trash, you might not even make game, despite the fact that an eight-card fit has been established. Matters gets worse when responder holds a mere five-card suit.

The problem is solved if opener stops obsessing about high card points and looks at his hand from the perspective of useful cards. Compare the two example hands: both were opened 2NT and, after the 3♡ response, were transferred to 3♠.

Hand 1 was:

♠ A 10 3   ♡ A 9 7 5   ◇ A 9 7 3   ♣ A K

This is a rock, despite being a six-loser 19-point hand. You have a known fit with partner (at least 5-3), with all suits controlled, all four aces and a king under an ace. This hand contains five assured cover cards, usually the maximum number possible. (If more is known about the two hands, it's possible to have six covers. For example:

♠ K Q   ♡ K Q 7 5   ◇ A 9 7 3   ♣ A K 3

if partner is known to have both spades and hearts.)

Hand 2 was:

♠ J 3   ♡ K Q J 8   ◇ A J 7 5   ♣ A K Q

This is much less interesting. Although your personal Losing Trick Count is still only five losers, your cover-card value for partner is much weaker. You have only three assured cover cards and no known fit. This is a radically different hand than the first one. Opener should be the one to distinguish between these hands.

The solution is for opener to cuebid immediately if he has the rock hand. With five cover cards, plus a fit, opener should usually cuebid. The approach I prefer, and suggest, is that opener, with a powerhouse raise, should cuebid the cheapest suit in which he holds 1½+ controls (K-Q-x or better). Four of the major would show a powerhouse response without a side 1½+ control holding (no A-K, A-Q or K-Q combinations). A 'powerhouse raise' typically shows a hand with at least five assured cover cards, plus body. Over a transfer to spades, such a hand would be:

♠ K Q 4   ♡ A Q J 3   ◇ A 9 8 6   ♣ A 10

If you like, opener can cuebid 3NT to show a powerhouse raise in the suit that is one-under the trump suit, thereby enabling responder to retransfer the contract to opener. For instance, if the transfer was to spades (3♡), opener might bid 3NT to show 1½+ controls in hearts, which retains responder's ability to bid 4♡ as a retransfer to 4♠.

A similar concept appears to have been used in the 2005 Seniors Bowl. Portugal reached a nice slam at one table, for a 10-IMP gain on these hands (rotated):

WEST	**EAST**
♠ K 10	♠ A Q 9 5 3
♡ 10 8 4	♡ A 6
◇ A Q 9 8	◇ J 7 4 3
♣ A J 9 8	♣ K Q

West opened 1NT, a fair bid in first seat because of the five controls and great intermediates. East transferred to 2♠ and then bid his second suit, 3◇.

West, realizing the value of his diamond honors and body, cuebid 4♣. Since 3♠ would establish spades as trumps, 4♣ can be nothing but a super-acceptance of diamonds and a cuebid.

East liked 4♣, so he bid 4♡, presumably RKCB for diamonds, as the out-of-focus major. West responded 5◇ (two keycards, plus the diamond queen) and the slam was bid.

More on Flag Bids

Many auctions get to a high level before a strain has been agreed. When this occurs, Flag Bids are extremely important assets. Flag Bids are used whenever only two logical strains exist and there is insufficient space to handle the problem without Flag Bids. Furthermore, Flags might be akin to a Last Train bid (invitational or better) or used as RKCB bids, identifying the suit of interest.

Flags for Minors

If the minors are in contention, two types of Flag Bids can occur, namely Flags below 3NT (akin to Last Train bids) or Flags above 3NT (RKCB Flags). Two examples will explain this concept.

First, suppose that 1NT-3◇ conventionally shows a minor two-suiter with game-forcing values. Opener can specify the minor of interest below 3NT by bidding 3♡ with clubs or 3♠ with diamonds. Similarly, if 1NT-2♠ is Minor Suit Stayman, opener might be allowed to bid 3♡ with a stunning club fit or 3♠ with a stunning diamond fit. Other situations should be discussed, but I generally use these flags whenever a minor two-suiter is shown in response to a 1NT opening.

Second, consider an auction where both minors are in contention for slam and the last bid is at the four-level in a minor. If the last minor call was 4◇, with either minor possibly the agreed fit (but not a major), 4♡ would be RKCB for clubs and 4♠ RKCB for diamonds. When 4♣ is the last call, with either minor (but neither major) offering the possible fit, some use the Redwood convention instead, where 4◇ flags clubs and is RKCB, and 4♡ is RKCB for diamonds. The partnership should discuss whether Redwood or ordinary Flag RKCB is used over 4♣, of course.

Flags for Majors

It is conceivable, I suppose, that an auction might occur where 5♣ is RKCB for hearts and 5◇ RKCB for spades. More important to spot, however, is the

Last Train Flag of 4♣ for hearts or 4♢ for spades, each showing a maximum or slammish hand. Some examples are fairly common.

WEST	EAST
2NT	3♢
3♡	3♠
?	

Opener could bid 4♣ to show a superacceptance (contextually) of hearts or bid 4♢ to flag spades.

WEST	EAST
1NT	3♠
?	

If 3♠ shows a major two-suiter, 5-5, with game-forcing values, Flags of 4♣ and 4♢ should obviously be used to enable opener to show a minimum hand or a maximum.

WEST	NORTH	EAST	SOUTH
2♢[1]	3♢[2]	pass	?

1. Weak.
2. Michaels (majors).

Here, 3♡ or 3♠ would be a simple preference. The jump to 4♡ or 4♠ could be a flier, especially at IMPs. To make a move toward slam, responder can use Flag Bids of 4♣ or 4♢.

FLAGS FOR MAJOR-MINOR SITUATIONS

Now things get trickier, but Flags are still useful in many major-minor situations. The most common of these is an opening of 2NT, followed by a Jacoby Transfer, followed by a minor at the four-level.

WEST	EAST
2NT	3♦
3♡	4♣
?	

A bid of 4♦ by opener flags clubs. Since 4♣ has been bypassed, the Flag is RKCB. If, instead, opener bids 4♠, hearts are flagged. Again, as 4♡ has been bypassed, 4♠ is RKCB. (4NT is needed as natural.)

WEST	EAST
2NT	3♡
3♠	4♣
?	

Here, again, 4♦ would flag clubs and be RKCB. Bidding 4♡ would flag spades; since 4♡ is below 4♠, however, it is a Last Train Flag, enabling a stop in 4♠ if responder was only mildly slammish.

WEST	EAST
2NT	3♡
3♠	4♦
?	

Here, space is limited. As no fit is assured, we need 4NT to be natural. Accordingly, the cheapest bid, 4♡, is a flag for diamonds. As 4♦ is bypassed, 4♡ is RKCB for diamonds. Due to spade concerns, this bid might be made with an actual spade preference, so a bid of 5♠ afterwards should be taken as a signoff. If opener wants to bid 5♣ over 4♦, however, this is a RKCB flag for spades. Alternatively, you could use 4NT RKCB for spades. If this is the agreement, opener must go through 4♡ to sign off in 4NT, hoping for an answer at or below 4NT.

WEST	EAST
2NT	3♦
3♡	4♦
?	

This is the worst of all flagging situations. Now 4♠ would be the RKCB Flag for diamonds and 5♣ the RKCB Flag for hearts. Each is costly in terms of space. Watch out for the 5♡ signoff after a 4♠ Flag.

The Golady Convention after 1 ◇ Openings

I have used the Golady convention with some partners to enhance certain cuebidding sequences that occur relatively frequently. We have agreed that in a 2/1 GF auction that starts 1◇-2♣, opener will use transfer rebids. Thus, in this sequence, opener would bid as follows:

2◇	=	four-card heart suit (as if he had rebid 2♡)
2♡	=	four-card spade suit (as if rebid 2♠)
2♠	=	agrees clubs
2NT	=	balanced
3♣	=	long diamond suit (as if rebid 2◇)

As you can figure out, the auctions are identical in all respects to 'normal' auctions, with three gains to one loss.

Two auctions that gain occur when responder can agree on a major at the two-level. For instance, assume that the auction is:

WEST	EAST
1◇	2♣
2◇¹	2♡

    1. Showing hearts.

Hearts have been agreed as trumps at the two-level. Now the same type of enhanced cuebidding is available as if the auction had been as follows:

WEST	EAST
1♡	2♣
2◇	2♡

Obviously, a similar auction allows spade agreement at the two-level.

The third auction that gains is where clubs can be agreed at the two-level with the 2♠ call:

WEST	EAST
1◇	2♣
2♠	?

Now responder can bid 2NT to show interest in a notrump contract, 3♣ to express doubt about a notrump contract with no serious slam interest, 3◊ to convert the agreed trumps to diamonds (clubs may have been false) and anything else is a cuebid, showing serious slam interest.

The sole loss is the inability to rebid 2◊ cheaply. All in all, the exchange is a fair one. Note that a rebid of 3◊ or higher over 2♣ still shows self-supporting diamonds.

Since we love this structure so much, we typically bid 2♣ to establish a game force on any hand with long clubs or even a hand which is balanced, possibly even a hand with one or both four-card majors. Accordingly, a simple major response to 1◊ is either too weak for 2♣, is unbalanced with short clubs or features a five-card major.

For example, consider a hand with four diamonds, four of a major and game-forcing values. All too often, you bid that major and then struggle to get diamonds into focus for a slam try. A 4441 hand is even worse in this respect. Had you simply bid 2◊ (inverted minors), the problem would be solved, but then perhaps you would have missed the major fit.

The solution is to bid 2♣. If opener shows your major, great! If not, bid 3◊ at your next turn to establish the diamond fit, game forcing. If partner bids 2♠, thinking he might be raising clubs, just revert trumps back to diamonds by bidding 3◊. Partner will understand.

A great example of the benefit of the Golady convention came up in the 2005 World Championships Seniors Bowl (hands rotated):

WEST	EAST
♠ A K J 6	♠ 9 8 3
♡ K J 8 2	♡ A Q
◊ 3	◊ A 9 7 2
♣ K J 9 2	♣ Q 8 7 5

At one table, East opened 1◊, West bid 1♡ and East bid 1NT. The club fit is too difficult to find in this auction and the slam was missed.

Consider the Golady option. West knows that a 2♣ call will accomplish several goals. If East has a major, he will bid one below that major, allowing West to 'accept the transfer', setting the major fit at the two-level in a game-forcing auction, with much more room available for cuebidding and no ambiguity as to whether cuebids are game tries or slam-going. Better yet, the club suit is not lost. So West bids it, forcing to game.

East has a roughly balanced hand, but in case 2♣ was based on a real club suit, he should bid 2♠, showing his support for clubs.

Back to West, for whom this is good news. Bidding 2NT would decline clubs, 3♣ would accept clubs weakly and 3◇ would agree diamonds. Bidding 3♡ would be a cuebid accepting clubs and showing slam interest — perfect. This is good news for East, as it likely fills in the ♡A-Q (a singleton being remote). However, since he lacks a spade control and good trumps, he bids 3NT, a non-serious 3NT implying poor trumps.

West is assuredly good enough now for at least a 4♣ call, waiting, with serious slam interest. As all of East's values are working, the non-serious 3NT earlier makes his hand a contextual powerhouse. He should now cuebid and arrive in slam.

Another example of the benefit of the Golady Convention came up in the 2000 Bermuda Bowl round robins:

WEST	EAST
♠ A 10 8 4	♠ 6
♡ A 9 4	♡ K Q 6
◇ K J 10 5	◇ A Q 9 7
♣ 10 2	♣ A 9 7 5 3

After East opens 1◇, West has the classic hand that shows why Golady can be so valuable. West starts the auction with the clear knowledge that a diamond fit exists if a spade fit does not. If there is to be a slam, however, West needs to find out about the club situation via cuebidding. A 1♠ response, if it fails to establish a spade fit, will critically damage any chance of establishing the diamond fit early enough for cuebidding. As you can see, however, 6◇ is a good contract if it can be reached.

With Golady, the auction is superior. West responds 2♣, establishing a game-force. East dispels any notion of a spade fit by bidding 2♠, showing a minor two-suiter. This induces West to bid 3◇, establishing the fit.

With a diamond fit discovered, East's hand has grown immensely. He starts with a 3♡ cuebid. This sounds like a notrump probe, but he will clarify his intentions later.

West has spades under control, but 3♠ shows this much better than 3NT. Bidding 3♠ shows a stopper that is also a control, whereas 3NT would imply something like Q-J-x-x in spades.

This helps East, but he is still concerned that the spade control might be the king and not the ace. Nonetheless, he can make a simple bid of 4◇, showing serious slam interest, clarifying that the 3♡ call was intended as a cuebid, denying two top club honors and showing good trumps (two top honors).

Surely West's hand, with K-J-10-5 in diamonds and two aces, is huge contextually. Accordingly, he should bid 4♡ as RKCB (cheapest out-of-focus major). Upon learning that East holds two keycards plus the diamond queen (5♢), West can visualize East as holding, at a minimum, something like:

♠ 6 2   ♡ K 6   ♢ A Q 9 7   ♣ A 9 7 5 3

That minimum, however, is hardly sufficient for a serious slam try. So, West should assume better shape, perhaps

♠ 6   ♡ K 6 3   ♢ A Q 9 7   ♣ A 9 7 5 3

at a minimum. Switch a club to a diamond, change the hand to 5-5 or add the heart queen and slam seems a fair bet.

Sure, this hand may boil down to a guess, partnership style and guts, but compare the amount of information West has here with the situation after the actual USA I auction, shown below:

WEST	EAST
	1♢
1♠	2♣
2♡	3NT

It is virtually impossible for West to make another bid now.

GOLADY AFTER 1♣ OPENINGS

To a degree, the same rationale applies to 1♣-2♣. A raise to 2♣, even if inverted, does not necessarily establish a fit anyway, especially if the partnership can open 1♣ on a doubleton.

The Golady rebid structure modifies easily to fit a club opening. If opener has a four-card major, he transfers with 2♢ or 2♡. With legitimate clubs, he bids 2♠. With a club-diamond reverse, he bids 3♣. With a balanced hand, he bids 2NT. In all events, responder is not forced beyond 3♣, the last escape point.

All the benefits of Golady are still present over a 1♣ opening. Primarily, responder can bid 2♣ with a four-card major, or both four-card majors, and can establish a game-force at the two-level if a major fit is found.

You might protest that this structure makes stopper exploration difficult. Not so. If opener lacks stoppers somewhere, he will usually be able to make a 2♠ call, showing a fourth club and establishing a fit if partner also has four or more clubs. From this point, stoppers may be explored.

9

CUEBIDDING WITH INTERFERENCE

When a Cuebid is Doubled

On occasion, a pesky opponent will double one of your cuebids as a lead-director. This can be quite annoying, as it suddenly creates the fear that all your efforts have gone to waste. We need rules to handle this problem.

After a lead-directing double of an artificial slam-going call, the standard agreement is as follows: redoubling shows first-round control of the suit; passing shows second-round control and bidding on denies control. This is too simplistic.

Take a simple example. I recently opened 2♣, heard 2◇ as a response (game-forcing, artificial) and bid 2♠. Partner raised to 3♠ and I bid 3NT (Serious 3NT). When partner cuebid 4♡, my RHO doubled.

WEST	NORTH	EAST	SOUTH
			2♣
pass	2◇	pass	2♠
pass	3♠	pass	3NT
pass	4♡	dbl	?

What are the critical cards for slam exploration at this point? Obviously, aces are great, but in this auction, I'm not going to be looking at the heart ace unless partner has a singleton. Who asks for a heart lead against a slam when missing both top honors in the suit? So if I'm unlikely to have the heart ace, what else is useful? Well, a heart singleton in my hand, or a second-round control, or a void. A queen is also huge, as it protects partner when his control is K-x-(x), but there has been little discussion of how to show it.

What are the key issues here? First and most obviously, partner may need help from me, especially if he has the unsupported heart king. Second, if he has the unsupported king, or even the ace, we may have a slam, yet opt to play a contract (if one exists and is viable) from partner's side in order to kill the lead-directional benefit. Any agreement should cater to all of these concerns. My suggestions follow.

REDOUBLE

If partner's cuebid showed a control, possibly the king, then a redouble by me shows the ace or a void. Most often, this enables partner to know that his singleton is not a loser or that I have control of the suit without a need for excessive trumping in his hand.

PASS

A pass denies a control. Traditionally, this has shown second-round control. However, I believe this treatment deprives partner of bidding room to explain his position when that's more important. When we pass (no control), partner has several options.

If he redoubles, partner shows that he has a control and can stand a lead through it, meaning the ace, a singleton, a void or the K-Q. In other words, redouble assures that we are still approaching slam in our agreed suit.

Without a solid control, partner might convert the auction to another strain. (Partner might, for instance, have continuing slam interest but hold a control in the threat suit that needs protection from the lead, meaning K-x-(x) in the opponents' suit.) This new strain could take several forms. First, partner may move the auction back to a suit he introduced earlier. Second, if notrump has not yet been bid, partner might suggest that strain. Third, partner might even introduce a new suit, as yet unbid, as a possible alternative strain. The idea is to find a contract that will let partner declare, since that will have better prospects.

Any call by partner in a suit that would be declared by the wrong side (and therefore would not protect the lead) should show first-round control in the threat suit and be a further cuebid.

CUEBIDDING ANYWAY

If you (the hand acting immediately over the double) continue to cuebid, you show a second-round control (singleton or king) or specifically the queen. The option of the queen is unusual, but sound. If partner has already shown a control (first- or second-round), he may need something else from you. Any of the three possibilities ensures that two immediate tricks will not be lost in the suit.

PUTTING IT ALL TOGETHER

Let's go back to the example auction from the start of this discussion. After I opened 2♣, partner bid 2◊ (artificial, game-forcing) and I bid 2♠. Partner raised spades (3♠) and I bid a Serious 3NT. Partner then cuebid 4♡ and RHO doubled.

WEST	NORTH	EAST	SOUTH
			2♣
pass	2◊	pass	2♠
pass	3♠	pass	3NT
pass	4♡	dbl	?

If I hold first-round control of hearts, I redouble. Partner will be able to guess my holding, usually. If he holds shortness as his heart control (singleton or void), he may safely assume that I hold the ace. If he holds the ace, he knows that I have a void. If he holds the king, he can safely assume that I have a void (so that K-Q offers a likely ruffing finesse), unless the double of 4♡ was psychic.

    Suppose, instead, that I pass. Partner will know that I have no heart control and no heart queen. With K-x as his control, partner will be concerned. He might sign off in 4♠. With good diamonds, however, he could bid 5◊, showing a real suit and serious slam interest, hoping 6◊ is an alternative. This is possible, because he will be declarer in a diamond contract.

In theory, partner might also suggest hearts as trumps, because neither of us, as of yet, has bid hearts (perhaps the double was based on a heart void).

If I pass (no control, no queen) and partner has first-round heart control, he might continue cuebidding, with any club, spade or notrump cuebid available. If, after I pass, partner has no available cuebid but he has first-round control of hearts or a singleton or K-Q, meaning a solid control, he can redouble. Normal cuebidding continues.

If I hold second-round control or the queen, I know we have hearts under control despite the double. At worst, partner has K-x, in which case even Q-x from me solidifies this control. So I just continue cuebidding over the double. Partner can trust that his heart cuebid, even if only K-x, was a real control in context.

WHEN THE OPPONENTS HAVE BID A SUIT PRIOR TO THE SLAM EXPLORATION

Suppose that the opponents are jamming us in a competitive auction. Partner opens 1♠, vulnerable against not, and his LHO butts in with 2NT, showing the minors. You make a good start with a 3◇ cuebid, setting spades as trumps and showing invitational or better values. Then opener's RHO gets particularly annoying and continues to 4◇. Now suppose you are slammish, without a diamond control. What next?

Cuebidding of controls is designed, in part, to ensure that the opponents do not take two tricks off the top. This becomes critical in a jammed auction with a known threat suit. General fit questions give way to bashing, as long as the opponent's suit is controlled. Control cuebidding should take precedence over all other questions. To best explain the rules for competitive cuebidding, I have provided examples of likely problems.

LAST TRAIN AS THE ONLY CUEBID

Let's consider a competitive auction where the opponents are bidding a suit two below ours. For example, after we agree that spades is our trump fit, the opponents compete in diamonds. In this scenario, the suit between ours and theirs is often the only cuebid available and is also the cuebid often interpreted as a Last Train cuebid. In this predicament, our Last Train meaning is that we have slam interest, but lack control of the opponents' suit.

For example, suppose you open 1♠, hear a Jacoby 2NT response from partner and RHO steps in with 4◇. That scoundrel! All is not lost. If you are slammish, you can pass, clearly forcing, and then pull partner if he doubles. This is a classic approach. But what about diamonds? What if you have two small diamonds?

The solution is simple. Passing and then pulling is different from a cuebid of 4♡, here interpreted as Last Train. One of the two should show a diamond control and one should deny a diamond control. Which makes the most sense?

To answer this question, assume that 4◇ will be raised to 5◇, further complicating matters, as even more space is consumed. If you start with a pass, partner won't know whether you are undecided or planning a pass-and-pull slam try. So it's logical for the ambiguous action to be the one that minimizes the likelihood of any further complications. A raise of this persistent interference is less likely if you have the ace or king of their suit, so logic dictates that the pass-and-pull slam try show control of their suit. Last Train, then, would show slam interest without control of their suit.

You may protest that a *shortness* control makes the pass-and-pull option more likely to face intervention, but we have to go one way or the other. This way seems best to me, in case the control is the ace or the king.

If the opponents bid 5◇ directly, then our 5♡ becomes a Last Train bid, asking for help in their suit. So, after 1♠-pass-2NT-5◇, 5♡ would be available to ask responder to bid slam if he holds a diamond control. With first-round control, of course, responder might explore a grand with further cuebidding.

WHEN LAST TRAIN IS NOT POSSIBLE

If the opponent's suit is right below ours (such as when they are competing over our spades by bidding hearts), much less room is available. Further, if we wait too long to clarify things, further interference may leave us with a problem. Suppose the auction begins:

WEST	NORTH	EAST	SOUTH
			1♠
pass	2NT	4♡	?

If I decide to cuebid 5♣ here and LHO bids 5♡, partner will not have any room to clarify the heart situation. This is a serious problem needing immediate attention.

Therefore, when available, an immediate bid of their suit should either ask for help in their suit (with other cuebids promising control in their suit) or show control in their suit (with other cuebids denying control in their suit). Again, a default agreement is needed, one which makes sense.

The traditional approach I learned as a bridge kid was for the bid of their suit to ask for help. Thus,

WEST	NORTH	EAST	SOUTH
			1♠
pass	2NT	4♡	5♡

is a sequence where opener shows slam interest without a heart control. This approach seems flawed, though, when you consider complicated auctions or auctions where the next bid is by a player with a relatively weak holding. Assume an auction where the opponents bid 4♡ in front of you and your announced values leave space for only one more keycard. If 5♣ showed a key club and heart control, you would be stuck, as having both might be impossible.

However, it is logical to have greater descriptive ability when you do have a heart control. Therefore, the default I learned as a kid actually does seem best. In such an auction, a cuebid of the opponents' suit, if immediately below our suit, asks for help in that suit. Notably, this parallels Last Train thinking and is consistent with the system generally.

Alternatively, a jump to five of our agreed suit, if a jump is possible, might take the place of the five-level cuebid, making the cuebid a simple control-showing bid. When this jump is not possible, the five-level cuebid in their suit should be control-asking.

Note that a cuebid of their suit asks for help there only if their suit is immediately below ours. Otherwise, a cuebid of their suit shows a control, as it normally would.

WHEN WE HAVE ALREADY CUEBID THEIR SUIT

If the opponents intervene in an auction where we have already shown control of their suit, the same principles apply as described above, with logical modifications depending on position.

A Last Train call by a person who already showed a control in the opponents' suit and who expects to be dummy shows an unprotected king in the opponents' suit, needing the ace or queen from partner (or shortness) if a slam is to make.

A Last Train call by a person who already showed a control in the opponents' suit and who expects to be declarer denies first-round control. If first-round control was already promised somehow, then the Last Train call denies having second-round control.

A Last Train call by the partner of the person who cuebid the opponents' suit, when he will be declarer, denies help for a hypothetical K-x from partner.

A Last Train call by the partner of the person who cuebid the opponents' suit, when he will be dummy, denies a second control in the opponents' suit.

WHEN THE OPPONENTS HAVE TWO SUITS

There is a rare occurrence where a unique agreement should be reached. I call this agreement 'Flag Last Trains'.

An example will explain this. Suppose you open 1♠, LHO overcalls 2NT for the minors and partner bids 3◇, which you agree as showing spade support and limit-raise or better values. What if RHO now bids 4♣?

In this situation, the opponents have two suits, either of which may supply a devastating lead against a slam. However, only two bids remain between 4♣ and bypassing 4♠, namely 4◇ and 4♡. If 4◇ shows a diamond control and if 4♡ shows a heart control without a diamond control, we have a lot of information about our diamond position, but no information about our club position. This is bad. I propose a better solution.

When the opponents have shown two suits, and when normal cuebidding will not allow us to explore both suits for controls, and when at least two cuebids exist below the next level of our agreed fit, the two calls immediately below our fit are flags for their two suits, each showing a need for control in the respective suit.

This may seem difficult to understand, but an example will make it clear.

WEST	NORTH	EAST	SOUTH
1♠	2NT	3◊	4♣
?			

Opener cannot cuebid normally to explore control of either minor. However, he does have two cuebids available — 4◊ and 4♡. The opponents have the minors. Therefore, using 'Flag Last Trains', opener can bid 4◊, the cheaper Flag Last Train, to show slam interest, with a need for control of the opponents' lower-ranking suit — clubs. Alternatively, opener can bid 4♡, the higher Flag Last Train, to show control of clubs, with slam interest, but ask for control of the opponent's higher-ranking suit — diamonds.

Note that 4◊ (the cheaper Flag Last Train) allows responder to reciprocate with a 4♡ call (the higher Flag Last Train) to show a club control (their lower-ranking suit) but no diamond help (their higher suit). Thus, in the example, opener could bid 4◊ with something like

♠ A K Q 5 3 2   ♡ A K Q   ◊ 8 5   ♣ 9 5

as a slam try, with *neither* of their suits controlled.

This same principle would apply at the five-level. Thus, if the auction was

WEST	NORTH	EAST	SOUTH
1♠	2NT	3◊	5♣
?			

opener still can use Flag Last Train bids at the five-level.

Back up. You might protest that all of this is unnecessary, since normal cuebidding would have solved the problem. After

WEST	NORTH	EAST	SOUTH
1♠	2NT	3◊	4♣
?			

4◊ by opener would show a diamond control and logically imply a need for a club control. Thus 4♡, Last Train, would logically deny a diamond control and therefore show a need for that diamond control and imply a club control. This is insufficient. As I illustrated, it is possible to have slam interest with neither of their suits controlled. Only Flag Last Train bids solve this problem.

Flag Last Train bids are not used if one partner or the other has already shown or denied control of one of the opponents' suits.

10

SOME DEALS FROM ACTUAL PLAY

If you have arrived at this point in the book, congratulations! You have worked hard to get through a mass of technical discussion and theory, and it's now time to wrap it all up by seeing how well the whole structure works in practice. I began our journey by describing how I had seen top-class partnerships struggle in complex slam auctions and how that experience had inspired me to begin thinking about cuebidding structures. In this respect, I often find it instructive to review the failings of the great players to see if my ideas might have solved their problems. It also heartens me to know that even those who actually play in the finals of major events slip up on occasion and that I might have done better — on those few deals, anyway — had I been given the chance. Over the entire day, they'll win, but could I gain on the odd deal? I love the thought of it.

I urge you to use what I have suggested as you consider a few of these deals where the world's best missed something. See if you, using these tools, could have found the solution that eluded the best of the best. Have fun!

In the Finals of the 2004 USBF Championship, both teams played 5♣ making six on these two hands:

WEST	EAST
♠ 3	♠ 10 9 2
♡ K 5 4 2	♡ A 7
◊ K 10	◊ A Q J 8
♣ K 10 9 7 6 2	♣ A J 4 3

One pair had an understandable problem when the opponents opened 1♠ and raised to 4♠ immediately. The other pair, however, had an uncontested auction that also missed the slam.

They started well. After three passes, East opened 1NT, apparently showing 15-17 HCP. West started with 2♣ (Stayman), East answering with 2◊. West completed the pattern with 3♣. East cuebid 3◊ and West cuebid 3♡. East then bid 4♣, which was raised to 5♣ to end the auction.

WEST	EAST
pass	1NT
2♣	2◊
3♣	3◊
3♡	4♣
5♣	

How should this have been bid?

When West introduces clubs, East should expect at least 5-4 pattern, with an unknown major. As West is a passed hand, slam exploration seems remote. Thus, East's 3◊ might be a probe for 3NT or a cuebid.

West's 3♡ might also be a probe for 3NT or a cuebid. To some degree, West should be considering 3NT if East has wasted spade values.

In the actual auction, East had the clear knowledge that 3NT could not be right and he bid 4♣. This was the error, in my opinion. East cannot want to play in 4♣. If 4♣ is passable, he is too strong for this call. If 4♣ is not passable, but a cuebid, East is wrong for this call, lacking two top trump honors. If 4♣ simply denies serious slam interest, East is too strong for this call also. Regardless of what 4♣ should show, 4♣ is not right. (I would take 4♣ as a cuebid, because 5♣ makes more sense as a denial of slam interest opposite a passed hand. If West were an unpassed hand, 4♣ would make more sense as non-serious and waiting.)

So East should bypass 4♣ to bid 4◇. Using the principles of cuebidding learned so far, this should logically deny a spade control, show a second top diamond honor and deny two of the top three clubs. This should also show serious slam interest.

What more does West need to know? One bad possible holding for East might be:

♠ 10 2   ♡ A 7 6   ◇ A Q 8 2   ♣ A J 4 3

So, it seems that West might need to know if the heart suit is doubleton or the diamonds stronger.

Neither question will be answered using RKCB. Additionally, West is not as concerned about the trump queen, since 4◇, showing serious slam interest, probably confirms either A-x-x-x or A-Q-x of trumps anyway. What should West do?

West actually has a rather simple call. He continues cuebidding with 4♠. This should show a spade control, of course. More importantly, it should express continuing slam interest without the ability to take over. In other words, Last Train ("I need something more").

What should East think now? Whether the doubleton heart or the solid diamonds is the key, he needn't worry; he has both. West cannot be concerned about trump solidity or he would have used 4♡ as RKCB to answer that question. Thus, the lack of the club queen, replaced by a third diamond honor and a doubleton heart, is powerful. Bidding 6♣ should be automatic.

Another interesting deal came up in the semifinals of the 2004 USBF Championships. Perhaps the most interesting part of this deal was that Meckwell missed a nearly laydown slam on these cards:

WEST	EAST
♠ A 9 3	♠ K 4
♡ A K Q 10 3	♡ J 9 6 5
◇ 10 4 3	◇ A 8 6
♣ Q 9	♣ A K 8 6

The auction was as follows:

WEST	EAST
	1◇
1♡	2♡
4♡	

Meckstroth made a Nebulous Diamond opening on the East hand; Rodwell signed off in 4♡, apparently deciding that 15 opposite a limited opening was too remote for a slam try.

The Nebulous Diamond may have caused some problems for Meckwell on this deal. Consider a better auction using a standard 1♣ opening, followed by a heart bid and raise. The West hand is a tricky beast. By Losing Trick Count, West has seven losers. However, Q-x is often undervalued, as in a sense it converts a small diamond or spade loser to a non-loser if partner has A-K-x. A six-loser hand opposite a six-loser hand (a 'maximum minimum') would make slam. So, West should temporarily view his hand as 'slammish', especially when the Q-x is in partner's minor.

Suppose West cuebids 2♠. East has a clear acceptance of this game try, having a maximum for his simple 2♡ raise. Once that is decided, East should convert to slam-going analysis in case West was actually slammish. East can then cuebid 3♣.

West cannot be sure whether 3♣ is a further game try or a slam move, but he has a simple bid: 4♣ cannot be misunderstood. West has a club card, spade control and no diamond control, with interest in a slam.

East can visualize a worst-case scenario of something like

♠ A 9 3   ♡ A Q 3 2   ◊ 10 4 3   ♣ Q 9 2

except that this is hardly slammish. Can East visualize the slam? He does not need to. The simple reality is that West's 3♠ call, followed by the 4♣ call, ensures that all controls shown so far are working. With a maximum for his 2♡ call, East trusts West (a noble thought for us all) and embarks on the slam.

Meckwell could have resolved this problem deal if East, after 2♠, had been obliged to identify his 'normal' minor opening when holding two of the top three honors in that suit. In other words, Meckwell could have the same auction if East were able to bid 3♣ over 2♠ on a hand with which a standard bidder would have opened 1♣. I have no idea how they handle this. In any event, Eric decided not to try for a slam with the West hand, which, considering some of the collections this pair opens, perhaps is not surprising.

However, we have unearthed an interesting idea that has applications in other situations. For example, auctions may occur where a partnership uses a 'nebulous' opening, in the sense of uncertainty about the minor suits. The simplest example is any notrump opening. Had the point-count been different, the opening bid would have been one of a minor, but opening 1NT leaves the minor suits 'in the dark'. Accordingly, auctions might occur where the 1NT opening is deemed 'nebulous' and an initial minor cuebid should follow the same principle just described as a suggestion for Meckwell.

Here's an example. You open 1NT and partner transfers to hearts. After you simply bid 2♡, partner bids 3◇, which you play as game forcing and artificial. You now bid 3♡, setting trumps, and partner cuebids 3♠. You are not contextually 'serious', but you want to cooperate with a minor call. The auction so far:

WEST	EAST
1NT	2◇
2♡	3◇
3♡	3♠
?	

What now? Arguably, this is a situation where the 'nebulous' 1NT opening calls for identification of the minor of choice had you opened a minor. Thus, 4♣ would be a cooperative cuebid showing two of the top three honors in clubs and clarifying that you would have opened 1♣ if the HCP count was slightly less. Bidding 4◇ would show the same thing, but with diamonds.

The next deal is rather amazing in that neither team found this laydown slam in the quarterfinals of the 2004 USBF Championship:

WEST	EAST
♠ Q 9 7 2	♠ 5
♡ K 8	♡ A Q 7 5
◇ A 6 4	◇ K 3
♣ A 5 4 3	♣ K Q J 10 7 2

At both tables, with West as dealer, the auction started 1♣-1♡. At one table, South intervened with 2♠, raised to 3♠. East then leaped to 5♣ to end the auction. This seems a tad wimpy, but the interference made the auction difficult.

WEST	NORTH	EAST	SOUTH
1♣	pass	1♡	2♠
pass	3♠	5♣	all pass

The other table had much less interference. South bid only 1♠ and North did not raise. This allowed East to cuebid 2♠, hear 2NT from partner and bid 3♣. 3NT came from West, which ended the auction.

WEST	NORTH	EAST	SOUTH
1♣	pass	1♡	1♠
pass	pass	2♠	pass
2NT	pass	3♣	pass
3NT	all pass		

This latter auction is faint-hearted, to say the least. First, East should splinter to 3♠ after 1♠ was passed to him. If West then bids 3NT, East is still strong enough to take one last stab at the slam, cuebidding 4♣ (two of the top three honors). West should cooperate by cuebidding 4◇, which clarifies the diamonds for East. As hearts have been ruled out as trumps, West could bid 4♡ as RKCB for clubs, but his sole issue is the location of the heart king. So 4♠, bypassing RKCB, should be Last Train, clearly requesting that card, and 6♣ is easily reached this way.

The actual auction is not a bad alternative, up to when 3♣ was raised to 3NT. If East wanted extra spade stoppers, he could have bid 3♠ after 2NT, so 3♣ must have been a slam try. West was not entitled to assume that slam was failing. He has great cards, despite the minimum. If he cuebids 3◇ instead, see how the auction develops. East now knows that his diamond king is protected and a trick; no diamond losers. East cuebids 3♡ to show two top heart honors.

West might now argue, persuasively, that he should sign off in 3NT, but his initial 3◇ cuebid helped East just enough to justify a 4♣ call, showing two top club honors and serious slam interest. This will yield a nice 4♡ call from West and the slam is again bid.

WEST	NORTH	EAST	SOUTH
1♣	pass	1♡	1♠
pass	pass	2♠	pass
2NT	pass	3♣	pass
3◇	pass	3♡	pass
3NT	pass	4♣	pass
4♡	pass	6♣	all pass

This next deal from the 2004 Spingold semifinals was played in 3NT at one table and in 5◇ at the other (hands rotated):

WEST	EAST
♠ A J	♠ K Q 4
♡ 8 2	♡ A 9 6
◇ A K Q 10	◇ J 7 6 3 2
♣ A 9 7 6 5	♣ 10 8

Here's how I think the bidding should go. After two passes, West opens 1♣, the opponents passing throughout. East responds 1NT and West reverses into 2◇.

East loves the 2◇ call and can cuebid 2♡, ostensibly seeking a notrump contract. West, with a great hand if partner can offer support for diamonds, cuebids 2♠, hoping 2♡ will prove to have shown a heart control. Assuming that the cuebid shows the ace of spades, East has a fairly good picture of West's hand already. West should have at least 5-4 in the minors, with the spade ace. This reduces the major losers to zero. Depending on West's exact minor holdings, slam is certainly possible. Unfortunately, East cannot contribute anything to the minor picture except a doubleton club. He completes his description by bidding 3◇, forcing game, probably denying a club notrump control and certainly a club slam control and denying a second heart control. The auction so far:

WEST	EAST
1♣	1NT
2◇	2♡
2♠	3◇
?	

West has heard enough to move toward slam now. With only five losers and very strong diamonds, the onus should be on West to make that stab. However, West cannot cuebid 4♣, as this would show two club controls (he opened 1♣).). Thus, West bids 4◇.

East now has strong indication that West has great trumps — why else be slammish? Thus, East should be able to use RKCB, 4♡, safely. The response is 4NT, clearly four. This looks like, at worst,

♠ A 2   ♡ 3 2   ◇ A K ? 4   ♣ A ? 4 3 2

the key being the trump queen. Now 5♣ is bid to find out. The cold slam is reached. The complete auction:

WEST	EAST
1♣	1NT
2◇	2♡
2♠	3◇
4◇	4♡
4NT	5♣
6◇	pass

Let's move to the 2003 Bermuda Bowl finals. On this deal, both teams missed a possible slam:

WEST	EAST
♠ 8	♠ J 9 5 3
♡ A K Q 9 7 5 2	♡ J 10 4
◇ J 4	◇ A Q 8 7
♣ K 10 6	♣ A 9

One team had difficulty when West opened 4♡. Whether his bid was meritorious or not, it happened to be an unfortunate one for this deal, as East could not justify making a bid past game.

The other team had a chance. After a pass from South, West opened 1♡, North doubled and East bid 2NT, apparently setting trumps. The opponents passed thereafter. The 2NT jammed the bidding and, despite my best efforts, makes finding the slam extremely difficult. Their next two bids were fine: West cuebid 3♣; East cuebid 3◇. At this point, West bypassed 3♡ (which may not have been forcing) to cuebid 3♠. East understandably signed off — although he probably should have made a cooperative cuebid of 4♣ on the way. This would help West and perhaps convince him to take the plunge.

Assuming they start 1♡-dbl, bidding 2NT seems flawed if it can be bid on poor three-card trump support and a balanced hand. Suppose that East had started with a redouble instead.

In practice, South will likely elect to escape into 1♠. West can now make a cute call. If West jumps to 3♠, it seems to me this ought to show a singleton spade and a long heart suit. This would be like a 1♡-3♡ start, with the addition of a singleton spade.

East needs little more information than this. He expects opener to have about a five-loser hand, long trumps and a singleton spade. On the auction, East also expects the diamond finesse to work, giving him at least three cover cards. Accordingly, he can establish hearts as trumps by cuebidding 4♣.

This helps West tremendously, as he probably expected his club king to be a doubtful asset. However, needing diamond help, he must logically sign off in 4♡. Back to East.

East now knows that the heart slam will depend on solid hearts and a diamond finesse (probably working). Since it is reasonable for East to expect to produce four covers, the fourth in the form of a club ruff, he bids 4NT and the rest is easy. Note that the lack of a diamond control from West was actually a benefit for East. His diamond finesse position is more valuable, as he is entitled to expect solid trumps from partner.

Our complete auction:

WEST	NORTH	EAST	SOUTH
			pass
1♡	dbl	redbl	1♠
3♠	pass	4♣	pass
4◇	pass	4NT	pass
5♠	pass	6♡	all pass

Another deal from the 2003 Bermuda Bowl finals was bid to slam by one team, but not the other, for a great swing when the slam made.

WEST	EAST
♠ A	♠ K 7 6 3
♡ K J 10 9 7	♡ A
◇ A 8 2	◇ K J 10 5
♣ 10 9 8 5	♣ A Q J 2

After a 1♡ opening and 2♣ response at both tables, the auctions diverged. The team that failed to reach slam seems to have done so because West delayed raising clubs, opting instead to rebid hearts. At the other table, West raised, inducing an immediate leap to 4♠ as RKCB for clubs.

A slower auction might also have been used. After 3♣ from West, East could simply cuebid 3◇. This ambiguous cuebid is possibly slam-going and possibly a notrump probe. East could always bid 4♠ (RKCB) later, because 3◇ establishes the possible strains as notrump, clubs or even hearts. Opener has a minimum hand with a spade stopper and should probably cooperate with a 3NT call. East will then know that West has at least a protected spade queen, and may have the ace. Thus, 3NT was inadvertently a non-serious cuebid of a spade value from East's perspective.

The notrump game is spurned by East, who cuebids 4♣ to show serious slam interest and good trumps. West can then cuebid his diamond control, 4◇. This leads East to the same conclusion as before, and 4♠ is whipped out, RKCB for clubs.

WEST	EAST
1♡	2♣
3♣	3◇
3NT	4♣
4◇	4♠...

This gets to the same spot as the pair who simply launched into RKCB over the initial club raise. The benefit of the slower auction, however, is the possibility of finding West with a hand like:

♠ A 2   ♡ K 9 7 4 2   ◇ A Q   ♣ K 10 9 8

Thirteen tricks seems easy on this layout. However, a jump to 4♠ over 3♣ won't pinpoint the ◇Q. Perhaps 1♡ was limited in some way, so that this hand was not possible in their system. For those of us who use regular old 2/1 GF, this hand is distinctly possible. What would the auction be after 3◇ from East if West does have that hand?

West would be serious about slam possibilities and would cuebid 3♠, denying two top heart honors, promising a spade control and showing serious minor slam interest. East could then cuebid 4◇, which we defined as showing good clubs (he bypassed 3NT) and a diamond control (4♣ would show good clubs without a diamond control). West could then bid 4♠ as RKCB for clubs, finding out about the heart ace. Next, 5♠ would ask for a specific king, with 5NT used to describe the king in the asking suit (the spade king). Counting twelve tricks easily, West could reasonably assume that either a third spade winner exists or two heart ruffs can be arranged or diamonds will come home. He would bid 7♣, making.

From the semifinals of the 2003 Bermuda Bowl comes this next deal, where only one of four teams found the slam (hands rotated):

WEST	EAST
♠ 10 5 4	♠ A K 3
♡ A K Q 5 3	♡ J 10 7 6
◇ 9 8 3 2	◇ A
♣ K	♣ J 10 9 4 3

Assuming a 1♡ opening from West, I strongly dislike 2NT from East. Things are much easier if East simply sets a 2/1 GF with a 2♣ call. Cuebidding sequences show to great advantage when the hand has poor trumps and an unusual pattern.

Opener has a problem over 2♣, because his hand offers a horrifyingly poor choice of rebids. 2◇ may be the best call and works wonders. As a rule, this type of auction suggests defaulting to a rebid below your major if at all plausible (even on a fragment, perhaps) in order to help partners who are trying to get to the agreed major fit at the two-level. This time, the plan works when East sets trumps with 2♡.

Anyway, opener has a simple cuebid of 3♣. This shows good trumps (at least two top trump honors) and a club card. The fact that the king is singleton is of no importance — if partner has good clubs, the king will be a vital card.

East continues this sequence by cuebidding his diamond card, also (humorously) singleton. Deals are like this, you see, when you play the big boys. This 3◇ cuebid does nothing to excite West, but he has an easy cuebid of 3♡ — all three top hearts, plus a club card — which completes the description of his hand.

East continues this sequence with great hopes by cuebidding 3♠. Unfortunately, this yields 4♡ from partner, but despite the signoff, East can still visualize a lot. Granted, West lacks a second club card, which would have been appreciated, but eleven tricks is a fair bet regardless. Twelve are possible if West has a good club honor (not the queen). So, East tries a sly maneuver — he bids 5♣.

As we discussed, a five-level call in our own side suit is RKCB, agreeing the original trumps, but with the 'keycards' including the king and queen of the side suit, not the trump suit. Here, knowing that hearts are solid, East has the luxury to try this. He hears 5♠, showing two keycards without the 'queen of trumps'. In other words, West has the known heart ace, the club ace or king, but not the club queen.

This is enough to make 6♡ a fair bet for East. East can visualize five heart tricks from West, two spade tricks himself and the diamond ace, for eight top tricks. At least one diamond ruff is probably assured, for a ninth trick.

If opener has even K-x-x of clubs, the slam makes when the queen is in the right spot — three additional club tricks come home. Give opener ♣A-x-x and the slam is 75%, it seems. Give opener A-x and clubs offer more chances, with a second diamond ruff in reserve. All of this leaves out the possibility of setting up the diamond queen as an additional trick (if West happens to hold that card).

As it turns out, opener has the worst holding, singleton king of clubs, with no diamond card at all. Nevertheless, a successful ruffing finesse in clubs will pull in the twelve tricks he needs to make the slam.

Viewing all possibilities, East was justified in seeking the club ace or king — the slam seems to be making more than 50% of the time it is bid in this auction.

The full auction:

WEST	EAST
1♡	2♣
2♦	2♡
3♣	3♦
3♡	3♠
4♡	5♣
5♠	6♡

This next deal took place in the round-robin event of the 2005 Bermuda Bowl, during the China-Portugal match, and ended with neither side reaching slam (hands rotated):

WEST	EAST
♠ A K J 9 7 4	♠ Q 10
♡ A	♡ Q 5 3
♦ A K 10 9 7	♦ Q 8 2
♣ 6	♣ J 10 4 3 2

At one table, the auction started as expected:

WEST	EAST
1♠	1NT
3◇	3♠
?	

The failure was the continuation. West knew that he had serious slam interest, no matter how weak 3♠ sounded. Accordingly, he cuebid 4♣. Looking at an unappetizing collection of queens and jacks, East signed off in 4♠ and then in 5♠ over West's last try of 5♡.

Now, back up a bit. Over 4♣, East had an easy solution. Using our approach, he could cuebid 4◇ to show one of the top three diamonds. This would be great news to West, who could simply launch into RKCB, bidding 4NT. Upon finding out that no club ace was offered (5♣ unless 1430), opener could ask for the trump queen, find it and the slam would be bid.

In that same match, eight deals later, both teams again missed a slam on these hands:

WEST	EAST
♠ Q 10 8 3 2	♠ K 7 5 4
♡ K 2	♡ A 8 4
◇ A K 10 8 5	◇ Q 7 4
♣ 5	♣ A 9 2

East opens 1◇, hears 1♠ from partner and raises to 2♠. Back to West, who apparently failed to recognize the quality of his hand. With an amazing diamond suit as a secondary fit and only five losers, slam is eminently plausible. Cuebidding is designed for these very deals. Granted, traditional HCP analysis suggests that slam is not making, but this deal shows the flaws in that thinking.

West should plan ahead on this one. He wants to show serious slam interest, but if he starts with 2NT, he will restrict his chances. A later 3NT call may be to play after the initial 2NT. So West starts with a simple 3♣ call, ostensibly a second-suit game try. He will clear that up later when he continues past 3♠.

Suppose East judges his hand unworthy of a game-try acceptance and signs off in 3♠. This is sent back to him with a 3NT call. Now East knows two things. First, West is serious about slam. Second, West's 3♣ call was actually a cuebid.

So now East cuebids 4♣, as requested. When West cuebids 4◊ over this, East should cuebid 4♡, just to be cooperative. Even if West signs off in 4♠, three keycards opposite serious interest is huge and East should not settle for 4♠. The 4♡ cuebid, however, should satisfy West that slam is a good bet.

Not every example I want to show you features getting to a slam the experts missed. Sometimes good technique protects the game bonus by not getting too high. On the next deal, from the 2005 Bermuda Bowl round robins between USA 2 and Italy, both teams ended up in 5♡, down one. Can we do better? (Hands rotated)

WEST	EAST
♠ A K J 8 3	♠ Q 9 6
♡ Q 7 5	♡ A K 8 4 3
◊ 10 6	◊ Q J 9 7
♣ A K 8	♣ J

The auction should be fairly predictable, to a point. West opens 1♠, hears 2♡ game-forcing and raises to 3♡. What next?

East has a simple 3♠ cuebid, showing a spade card (queen or higher). Remember from our earlier discussion that this bid does not shift trumps back to spades. You do not bounce back and forth between majors. We are not that finicky.

Opener will probably have little problem deciding that he is serious, as the spade queen is a huge contribution from East. Opener bids Serious 3NT. Back to East. East has a club control (shortness), so 4♣ is an easy continuation. Back to West.

This is the critical moment. West has bid Serious 3NT. Accordingly, Last Train is available for West. He can, therefore, make a great call of 4◊, contextually suggesting the need for a diamond control.

What more needs to be done? East, lacking a diamond control, signs off in 4♡. All the excitement in the world does not remove the ace or king of diamonds from the opponents' hands.

WEST	EAST
1♠	2♡
3♡	3♠
3NT	4♣
4◊	4♡

The next deal is particularly interesting from the perspective of planning. In the quarterfinals of the 2005 USBF Championships, only one team found the slam on these cards:

WEST	EAST
♠ J 9 8 4 2	♠ A 10 7 3
♡ A K Q 7 4	♡ 8
◊ 7 3	◊ A K Q 4
♣ Q	♣ A 9 8 7

The auction starts with 1♠ from West and East has the first interesting decision. He plans on setting spades as trumps. With a singleton heart, he is fairly confident that whichever minor he chooses to respond in, West's next call will be 2♡. This would be tremendous, saving a world of space.

East should think further than that. Ultimately, he may be able to cuebid diamonds and clubs. If his initial response is 2♣, it will take a long time to show diamond strength and club cuebids will initially be unavailable. If, however, his response is 2◊, he will be able to show two of the top diamonds immediately (with his first diamond cuebid), possibly show A-K-Q of diamonds and will be able to show the club control sooner. Thus, 2◊ is the best calculated call.

As expected, opener bids 2♡ next. East sets trumps with 2♠. Back to West. West would have liked to make a Picture Splinter of 4♣, but his spades are too poor. West resigns himself to bidding 2NT, showing poor trumps.

East now cuebids 3♣. Step one reached — cuebid the club control. West cuebids 3♡, denying honor help in diamonds (no kidding), but showing two top heart honors.

Back to East. He can bid 3NT, showing serious slam interest and poor trumps (he bypassed 3♠). This is discouraging to West, but he should cooperate anyway, in case East has his actual hand. West cuebids 4♣, showing a club control.

East may opt to continue cuebidding at this point, bidding 4◊ to show two of the top three diamond cards. This is great, because in practice it enables West to show his solid hearts by cuebidding 4♡. What more does East need? RKCB shows that the spades have some gaps, but 6♠ should still be a fairly good shot. Worst case scenario is ♠8-6-5-4-2 from opener. In that event, the slam makes on a 2-2 trump split. If West holds the spade jack, it will improve their chances...

The complete auction:

WEST	EAST
1♠	2◇
2♡	2♠
2NT	3♣
3♡	3NT
4♣	4◇
4♡	4NT
5◇	6♠

Here's another interesting deal from the 2005 USBF Bridge Championships, hands rotated, where a slam was missed:

WEST	EAST
♠ A 8 7 5	♠ K Q 9 6
♡ K J 9 6	♡ A 10 4
◇ A Q	◇ J 10 9 8 2
♣ A J 4	♣ 10

West, in second seat, will often open 2NT. Seven controls is a fine basis for an upgrade, taking the hand to a 20-count. Furthermore, many experts agree to open 2NT in first or second seat when holding a good 19 HCP in order to give themselves an extra chance of declaring a notrump contract. This hand is ideal for that purpose as well.

If the opening bid is 2NT, East will use whatever form of Stayman he has available. Assuming it is 3♣ Puppet Stayman, West will respond 3◇ and East will bid 3♡ to show spades. West can then agree spades with a 3♠ call. Bidding 3♠ tends to deny anything special, as opener could have superaccepted spades by cuebidding 4♣, 4◇ or 4♡.

East should now cuebid 3NT, Serious 3NT, because his hand is huge and because he wants to hear a 4♣ call. He has a plan to launch something truly sublime, as well. When he hears 4♣, step two of the secret plan is put into action: he cuebids 4♡ to deny a diamond control and show a heart control. Note that, even after a Serious 3NT, responder's 4♡ should be taken as legitimate, because the strength of the deal is extremely tilted to West. Accordingly, East continues describing his hand.

If West takes over here, as he should, the slam should be reached.

WEST	EAST
2NT	3♣
3◊	3♡
3♠	3NT
4♣	4♡
4NT…	

From the 2005 Spingold semifinals comes this deal, where only one team reached the slam (hands rotated):

WEST	EAST
♠ Q 9 4	♠ A
♡ A K Q J 7	♡ 10 4 2
◊ K 10 3 2	◊ A 7 6
♣ Q	♣ K J 9 8 6 5

After West opens 1♡, East responds 2♣ and West rebids 2◊. East sets trumps with 2♡.

Now West cuebids 3♣ to shows no spade control, good trumps and one of the top three club honors. Since West has no spade control, East knows that West has at least two spades, reducing his club count to a singleton or doubleton, possibly A-x, Q-x, singleton ace or singleton queen. Any such holding is interesting.

East continues with the obvious 3◊ call, showing a diamond card (partner's suit). Since West denied a spade control, this call also promises at least second-round spade control. Note that East could not make a 4◊ Picture Jump, because his diamonds are too weak.

West can now cuebid 3♡ to show the third top heart honor. This is a relief to East, of course, who can rely on the suit to be at least ♡A-K-Q-5-3.

East, having already shown a spade control, cuebids 3♠ to confirm first-round control. The auction so far:

WEST	EAST
1♡	2♣
2◊	2♡
3♣	3◊
3♡	3♠
?	

At this point, West has an issue. If he had the diamond queen, he could cuebid 4◇ to promise two diamond cards, solidifying the suit after East's 3◇ call earlier. With

♠ 3 2   ♡ A K Q 5 3   ◇ K Q 3 2   ♣ Q 2

a 16-point hand, his entire hand would be on the table. Whether the 4◇ cuebid is 'serious' or 'not serious', it would finish his description. Whenever one cuebid completes the description of your hand, choose it rather than bidding the ambiguous Serious 3NT. For that matter, if a simple cuebid would complete your description, bidding 3NT denies holding that hand (redundancy avoided). It would show a better hand or a different one.

On the actual deal, however, bidding 4♣ is wrong, as that would tend to show something like:

♠ 3 2   ♡ A K Q 5 3   ◇ K 5 3 2   ♣ A Q

Bidding 4◇ would also be wrong, for the reasons already explained, and 4♡ is a terrible call, a signoff on 17 HCP. Thus, West is semi-forced to make a Serious 3NT call to suggest holding good stuff, in whatever way that may be interpreted. It should be interpreted as 'good stuff not otherwise biddable with one bid'.

East should figure it out. If West held two top diamond cards, two top clubs cards and all three top hearts, he would have taken over by bidding 4NT. With only two top clubs, he would have bid 4♣. With only two top diamonds, he would have bid 4◇. Therefore, by deduction, West must have something like the ace of diamonds, possibly Q-x-(x) of spades, and possibly a singleton club honor. Little more needs to be known. Time for RKCB.

This deal illustrates a great principle that should be restated: 3NT is not a cuebid designed purely to express happiness. It is a cuebid designed to handle real bidding issues, expressing enthusiasm along the way.

Sometimes, a Serious 3NT call is a demand bid directing partner to tell more. Contextually determined, it is a captainship grab. It usually occurs when one partner is expected to be stronger or when the other partner is expected to be able to complete his description fairly rapidly.

Sometimes a Serious 3NT call handles a problem of unexpected general strength.

Sometimes, a Serious 3NT call describes an unbiddable hand which nonetheless has slam interest. As in the example here, to a degree, the Serious 3NT call might be no more powerful a call than a 'cooperative' cuebid, if the call is used to describe a 'missing' hand.

On this deal from the 2005 Bermuda Bowl semifinals, only one team reached the slam (hands rotated):

WEST	EAST
♠ K 10 9 7	♠ Q 3
♡ Q 10 7 2	♡ A K J 9 8 3
◇ Q 4 2	◇ A
♣ A 5	♣ K J 8 3

The failing auction started out fine. West passed in first seat (unusual in this event on this kind of hand) and the auction started with a third-seat 1♡ opening from East. West then bid 2♣, presumably Drury, although I am not sure whether their agreements defined 2♣ as four-card support (with 2◇ as three-card support) or just 3+ support. In any event, East next bid 3♣, apparently showing extra strength with a club suit. When West bid 3♡, East signed off in 4♡, a bid which lacked imagination.

East should have recognized that slam is eminently possible. Give West the lesser hand of

♠ K 6 5 2   ♡ Q 5 4 2   ◇ 8 7 3   ♣ A 4

and a slam is still essentially cold. Signing off in 4♡ was simply giving up on the auction.

East has a simple bid to seek slam. If East bids 3NT, this is Serious 3NT (serious slam interest), with an implied lack of a spade control (East did not cuebid 3♠). Now West can cuebid 4♣, which must show a club control directly (presumably the ace, due to his failure to make a splinter or a Flower Bid earlier). Inferentially, 4♣ also shows a spade control; otherwise, West would sign off in 4♡. This is likely to be an honor, based on his failure to splinter earlier.

At this point, the worst possible hand for West would be:

♠ K 6 5 2   ♡ 5 4 2   ◇ Q 8 7   ♣ A 4 2

With this hand, however, West would simply have raised the 1♡ opening to 2♡. Even adding the spade jack does not really change the ideal bid. Thus, we expect 2♣ to show something better. So the slam should probably be bid.

Note that knowledge of the fourth heart gives East some insurance. This is a particularly compelling argument for two-way Drury.

In the 2005 Bermuda Bowl finals, both pairs reached only 6♣ on this next deal, scoring up 940 when only 8 IMPs separated Italy and USA I. Could you have done better?

WEST	EAST
♠ 5 2	♠ A J 8
♡ A K Q 3	♡ 7
◇ A 9 5	◇ K Q 10 2
♣ 7 6 4 3	♣ A K Q 8 2

The auction at both tables started the same way. After a pass from North, East opened 1♣. South overcalled 1♠ and West doubled, North passing again. The auctions diverged at this point, but both roads led to a lesser Rome of 6♣. East for USA I opted for 3NT and West decided to bid on; Italy went for 2◇.

The Italian auction had more promise. After a rebid of 2◇ from East, West bid 2♠, assumed to be asking for a stopper for notrump. East showed it by bidding 2NT. (Apparently, a game-force was in effect.) West cuebid 3♠, of uncertain definition. This enticed North to double for some reason (North held two small spades), allowing East to redouble, presumably showing first-round spade control (as it would).

WEST	NORTH	EAST	SOUTH
	pass	1♣	1♠
dbl	pass	2◇	pass
2♠	pass	2NT	pass
3♠	dbl	redbl	pass
?			

This makes for an interesting start. West can now bid 4♣ to let East in on the secret trump suit. This allows East to cuebid 4◇ to show two of the top three honors in diamonds. Now 4♠ by West is RKCB for clubs, allowing him to find out about all five top minor honors and the spade ace. West's three top hearts, plus partner's spade ace, erase all major losers. The fourth club lets the suit be without a loser, except when clubs split 4-0. This same fourth club also covers the fourth diamond from East in case diamonds are not 3-3. Further, some 4-0 splits in trumps might be manageable, depending on East's club texture.

After this auction, getting to 7♣ should be easy.

On some deals, cuebidding might get you to an amazing slam. On the next deal, from the quarterfinals of the 2005 Bermuda Bowl, both teams declared 6♠, down two, when a different slam was making. (Hands rotated.)

WEST	**EAST**
♠ Q 9 8 7 3	♠ A 5 2
♡ K Q 5	♡ J
◊ Q 9	◊ A K J 7 6
♣ Q 9 2	♣ A K J 5

West opens 1♠, which produces 2◊ from East. With a flat 11-HCP hand, possibly not even worth opening, West bids 2NT. East sets trumps with 3♠, which doesn't remotely interest West. Nonetheless, he must show non-serious slam interest (a great understatement) and cuebid what he has. Bidding 4◊ denies a club control, but shows one of the top three diamond honors.

East has enough to move, of course, and launches into 4NT, RKCB. The 5♣ response is discouraging, showing no keycards. East now knows that the heart ace is missing as well as the spade king. What to do?

East has two options. One, he might sign off in 5♠, which gains 3 IMPs on the deal, since it goes down only one. Two, he can start to think. The 4◊ cuebid suggests that diamonds might be playable. We know we're off the ♡A and the ♠K, but since West opened the bidding, we have an assured 32-33 HCP. Partner must have the K-Q of hearts and the diamond queen for his opening, so bidding 6◊ seems in order. With the spade king well placed, 6◊ ends up being untouchable (not that anyone was leading a spade on this auction anyway).

You might note that the 4◊ cuebid did not really help much, because partner is unlikely to open with:

♠ Q J 9 8 7   ♡ K Q 5   ◊ 9 3   ♣ Q 9 2

Two teams that made it to the quarterfinals of the Bermuda Bowl did not see this. Indeed, given the general aggressiveness of opening bids at the international level these days, perhaps that hand would have merited a 1♠

bid. So West's actual hand seems well worth a 4◇ cuebid. Indeed, even if we change the East hand slightly to remove the heart jack, replacing it with a small heart, 6◇ still has merit after this auction, with the 4◇ cuebid being much more significant.

An extremely interesting auction might have avoided the failing slam that was reached at both tables in the semifinals of the Seniors Bowl at the 2005 World Championships, on this deal (rotated):

WEST	**EAST**
♠ Q 10 8	♠ K 7 2
♡ K 7 6 2	♡ A Q 10 3
◇ J 10 7	◇ A K 5
♣ K Q 4	♣ A 10 8

At one table, West opened a Nebulous 1◇ and East bid 1♡. After West raised this to 2♡, RKCB was used and the slam was bid, down one. At the other table, the contract was the same, but went down two tricks.

Can our tools help to avoid this slam? The simple solution might be to resist opening garbage 11-count hands. However, with a bit of technique, slam might be avoided even after a sub-minimum opening from West.

Suppose West opens 1♣. If the partnership uses Golady after 1♣ openings, East, with no five-card major, can bid 2♣, either game-forcing or at least invitational with support. West, using Golady rebids, introduces his hearts with 2◇, allowing East to agree trumps at the two-level, bidding only 2♡. This also confirms that we are in a game-forcing auction.

West hates his hand, but cooperation is key to good partnership bidding. (You'll lose a lot of partners by opening trash and lying later on. Sleep in the bed you made.) So West resigns himself to a cuebid of 2NT, directly showing poor trumps and inferentially denying a spade control. At least the message of ill tidings offers some relief.

East, holding a spade control and one of the top three clubs (opener's first suit), cuebids 3♣, showing both. He is hard to dissuade.

West cuebids 3♡, denying a diamond control, but showing one top heart honor.

Back to East. East bypasses 3♠ to deny first-round control (second-round control was already implied) and cuebids 3NT, showing serious slam interest. Holding 20 of the finest high cards points justifies this move.

West, not impressed yet (he never will be), finally gets a chance to cue-bid his clubs, 4♣, to show the remaining two club honors.

East can now cuebid 4◊, Last Train. West has little help to offer. The only possible additional features would be extra club length (which he lacks), the diamond queen (also lacking) and the spade queen. With all three, West should bid 4NT. With none of the above, 4♡ seems automatic. With two of the three, West could bid either 4♠ (spade queen plus either long clubs or the diamond queen) or 5♣ (long clubs plus the diamond queen). With only one, however, West does best by signing off in 4♡.

East cannot stand it and must ask again. Opposite as little as

♠ 10 8 3   ♡ K 7 6 2   ◊ 10 7   ♣ K Q J 4

6♡ would have play, requiring only 9 HCP from West. Bidding 4NT answers no questions, but 4♠ might. This is somewhat undiscussed, but a 4♠ call from East contextually acts like a general cuebid. Perhaps this could be called 'Serious Last Train'?

What should West do over 4♠? With his horrible hand, he will reject the invitation to bid 4NT as RKCB. With K-Q-J-4, he would be able to cuebid 5♣, so bypassing it must show ♣K-Q-x-x at best. Bidding 5◊ would imply a doubleton diamond, so 5♡ seems in order.

What can West have, from East's perspective? At best, West might have something like:

♠ Q J   ♡ K 7 6 2   ◊ J 10 7   ♣ K Q 4 2

With that hand, the Q-J of spades looks useful, as does the J-10 of diamonds, so he might well have bid 4NT. More likely is that he had a trashy 3-4-3-3 opening.

Imagining this layout, the best possible hand for West is now:

♠ Q J 8   ♡ K 7 6 2   ◊ J 10 7   ♣ K Q 4

Opposite that trash, the slam still seems a fair bet. It makes whenever the diamond finesse works, so long as hearts can be brought in. Reduce the hand slightly, taking away the diamond ten, and the slam is horrible.

Will this slam be bid anyway? Perhaps, but this delicate dance gives us a much better chance of stopping than simply blasting into RKCB.

In the finals of the 2003 Spingold, both teams threatened to bid the poor slam on this next deal, but one managed to stop with inferior information. The other team reached the hopeless slam to lose 13 IMPs. I suspect they bid it out of desperation, trusting to luck. The hands have been rotated:

WEST	EAST
♠ 6 4 2	♠ Q 7
♡ A K Q 6 3	♡ J 9 2
◇ Q 8 7 5	◇ A K J 6 3
♣ A	♣ J 5 3

After West opens 1♡, East bids 2◇ and West should bid 3◇. In actual play, however, both Wests jumped. At one table, the jump was to 4♣, a splinter, and seems a poor choice with a singleton ace and only one top diamond. At the other table, 3♠ was the call, possibly a psychic cuebid in hopes of stealing a slam.

In any event, after a saner 3◇, East should convert trumps to hearts by bidding 3♡. Granted, diamonds might be the right slam, but East has a terrible hand for the auction. Besides, 6◇ can always be bid later.

After 3♡, West can make any call above 3♠ that he desires. Whatever he picks will deny a spade control, so East, also lacking a spade control, has a simple signoff in 4♡.

An interesting slam was missed in the 2000 Vanderbilt finals by one team. An inferior (but making) slam was bid by the other team. This was the deal:

WEST	EAST
♠ A 5 2	♠ Q 10 8
♡ A 9 2	♡ K Q J 8 5
◇ A K 9 7 4	◇ Q 6 2
♣ K 10	♣ J 6

East opened 1♡ on that mess. West responded 2◇, followed by 2NT from East. West now set trumps with a 3♡ call. At this point, East apparently downgraded his hand to below an opener, or lacked tools, and signed off in 4♡. An undoubtedly disappointed West showed great trust by passing.

WEST	EAST
	1♡
2♢	2NT
3♡	4♡

East should not have acted so unilaterally. His great heart strength certainly merits simply bidding his hand out. Over 3♡, East should bypass 3♠ (no spade control), bypass 3NT (no serious slam interest, an understatement), bypass 4♣ (no club control) and cuebid 4♢ (showing one of the top three diamond honors).

The paucity of side values should convince West to be cautious. However, it also means that East is obliged to have heart honor strength. The best hand possible for East seems to be:

♠ Q 10 8   ♡ K Q J 8 5   ♢ Q J 6   ♣ Q J

The spade jack in the East hand might ensure the contract on a spade lead if the contract is 6♢.

Think about this further. What about clubs? Suppose partner is only slightly weaker, something like:

♠ Q J 8   ♡ K Q J 8 5   ♢ Q J 6   ♣ J 6

Now 6♢ will be safe from any lead, whereas a club lead might spell doom for 6♡.

The worst hand West can visualize for East is the hand that actually turned up. Much worse would be:

♠ Q 8 3   ♡ K Q 8 5 3   ♢ Q 6   ♣ Q 6 2

East is certainly entitled to use judgment, but hiding the diamond queen, with three-card support and great hearts, is questionable. West should expect East to bid 4♡ on many absolutely horrifying openers, justifying his slam drive when East does not sign off.

Once West settles on slam, he might leap to either 5NT or 6♢, whichever bid the partnership would take as choice of slams, as a hedge. 6♢ immediately seems sound. On the actual deal, 6♢ is cold on a club or spade lead from North. Any other lead merely forces a percentage play later, the logical one being a spade guess. On this occasion, North held the ♠K-J, so 6♢ would make.

No one found the slam on these cards in the 2005 Bermuda Bowl round robin (hands rotated):

WEST	**EAST**
♠ Q 8 6	♠ A K 10 4 3
♡ 10 6 3 2	♡ A K Q 7
♢ K 9 2	♢ Q 8 6
♣ A 9 8	♣ 3

When East opens 1♠ and West responds 2♠, constructive, East is entitled to expect a hand with three (or four) potential cover cards. With close to a four-loser hand, slam seems likely. Accordingly, East bids 3♡, ostensibly a real-suit game try, but actually intended as a move toward slam.

West unfortunately lacks the hand necessary for a Serious 3NT response. Although he has four-card heart support, he lacks three keycards. Change his diamond king to the ace and 3NT is his call. This would yield an easy slam bid by East, but more delicacy is needed on this deal.

Two plausible options exist for West. He could opt to raise to 4♡, showing support with a desire to try for ten tricks, or he could simply cuebid. However weak the hearts are, it seems best to focus the partnership on a switch to the 4-4 fit. Now East can be fairly confident of eleven or more tricks, depending on the precise nature of the minor-suit values. East will suspect that West holds an ace and a king on the side, but he will be unsure as to their locations. Knowing which king West holds will be critical to their slam chances.

The solution here is for both partners to think through East's initial options. With a void in diamonds, East probably would have used a splinter directly over 2♠. Since he did not do that, 5♢ by East now is probably not Exclusion RKCB; rather, it would be RKCB with the minor keycards being the diamond king and queen. If this is understood, the diamond king is located and 6♡ reached.

From the 2000 Bermuda Bowl round robin between USA I and Italy we have this gem. USA I missed the slam and forfeited 13 IMPs on this deal (hands rotated):

WEST	EAST
♠ K Q 7 6 4	♠ A 10 2
♡ 9 4	♡ A K 5 2
◊ A K 5	◊ J 10
♣ J 10 2	♣ A 9 8 6

The auction for USA I started nicely, with West opening 1♠, East responding 2♣ and West bidding 2◊. The 2◊ call was logical, as West (i) wants to enable East to raise spades at a lower level if that was his plan and (ii) has a two-honor fragment in diamonds, a holding that allows better cuebidding later if the suit is bid.

At this point, East lost focus by introducing hearts, muddling the auction to the point where finding the spade fit was delayed until most of the cuebidding space had vanished. East, in essence, preempted the partnership.

If East simply bids 2♠, the auction goes much better. West can now bypass 2NT (good trumps), which lets East know that the spades are solid at the top. West can also bypass 3♣ to deny as much as the club queen — bad news for East — and cuebid 3◊ to show two top diamond honors. Contextually, this carries the message that West also lacks the third diamond honor; otherwise West could have jumped to 4◊ (a Picture Jump Cuebid) or made a Picture Splinter of 4♣ or 4♡.

East is unsure where this is going, if anywhere, but he has no other call but 3♡, showing a heart control.

WEST	EAST
1♠	2♣
2◊	2♠
3◊	3♡
?	

West has shown all the relevant features of his hand. If he held a singleton club, he could now cuebid 4♣, as he has already denied a top honor in clubs. For that matter, he could also cuebid 4♡ to show a singleton heart. Instead, he signs off in 4♠, suggesting something like

♠ K Q 7 6 4   ♡ 9 4   ◊ ? ? ? ?   ♣ 10 2

maybe with another jack (except the diamond jack) and possibly with only three diamonds.

East, with J-10 of diamonds, expects that making twelve tricks will depend on diamonds. If opener holds A-Q-x-x or A-K-x-x, the diamond finesse, if working, will yield an eleventh trick, followed by a diamond ruff to clinch the twelfth. Ergo, slam will make often enough for East to venture a slam try. Accordingly, East uses simple RKCB to confirm that opener holds the diamond ace and then bids the slam.

As it turns out, West has the 'death' hand of a three-card diamond fragment. The ◇A-K-5 removes the need for the diamond finesse at Trick 11: a simple diamond ruff provides that trick. However, this holding also eliminates any chance of a Trick 12 from diamonds. Fortunately, West has the additional bonus of ♣J-10-2 — the slam will turn on one of two club finesses, which works.

Note that West was justified in his 2◇ call, way back, because of this unbiddable but probably useful surprise in clubs.

In the 2006 USBF championships, Soloway-Hamman and Bramley-Feldman both missed a slam that is easy to bid using my methods. (Hands rotated for convenience.)

WEST	EAST
♠ K J x x	♠ Q 10 x x
♡ 10 x x x	♡ —
◇ A x	◇ K Q x
♣ A K Q	♣ J 10 9 8 x x

At each table the auction went as follows:

WEST	EAST
1NT	2♣
2♡	3♣

West then showed some promise (not enough for East) with a 3♠ call, and each East signed off in 4♠ without even taking a stab at slam.

This hand affords a great opportunity to use the Empathetic Splinter. When East bids 3♣, he is known to have four spades and five or more clubs. West has a spade fit, with five covers in the two suits and no wasted values in hearts. He can show this with a jump to 4♡, an Empathetic Splinter.

East, knowing that West has no wasted values in hearts, a spade fit and five of the six missing top cards in spades, clubs and diamonds, simply bids 6♠.

Remember, the concept behind an Empathetic Splinter by an opening bidder is that he shows a double fit with five of the seven critical cards. The critical cards are the A-K-Q of the two suits and the ace of the suit not opposing the shortness. Thus, the leap identifies the potential fit so that responder knows whether there in fact is that secondary fit (meaning, where the secondary honors outside of the known trump fit are).

When responder's two suits are known, as here, the jump can identify the weakness. So in the auction above, 4♡ and 4♢ might each make sense as identifying weakness (with the ace in the other red suit as a critical card).

The slams missed by the experts never cease to amaze me. Consider this deal, which caused problems for USA 2 in the 2000 Bermuda Bowl (hands rotated):

WEST	EAST
♠ A 7	♠ J 10 5
♡ A 6 5	♡ K Q J 10 8
♢ A Q J 10 6 5	♢ K 2
♣ K 8	♣ Q J 4

This is clearly making 6♡ or 6♢. The Italians reached 6♢. Now look at where USA 2 ended up:

WEST	EAST
1♢	1♡
2NT	3NT

Assuming they start 1♢-1♡; 2NT, which I think is a serious underbid by West, what is East doing? He should bid 3♢, checkback for the major, as cuebidding will be easier with a fit.

West will respond 3♡. Now East can cuebid 4♢ to deny a spade control, deny a club control and show a diamond card. Alternatively, East can be aggressive and cuebid 3NT, showing serious slam interest without a spade control. He will hear 4♣ from West and can cuebid his diamond card. In either event, West should take over with a simple 4NT RKCB. Bidding 6♡ is then easy.

Slam was missed by one team in the 2000 Bermuda Bowl on the following deal. The auction started the same way at both tables.

WEST	EAST
♠ K J 9 6 3	♠ A Q 5 4
♡ K 10 9 7	♡ A 8
◊ A K	◊ J 9 3
♣ Q 7	♣ K 5 4 3

WEST	EAST
	1♣
1♠	2♠
?	

What would we do next?

West clearly has game-forcing values. More importantly, he has a six-loser hand, with Q-x in clubs. Q-x holdings often create strange additional tricks. In any event, almost every six-loser hand opposite an opener should be the subject of cuebidding and West needs to be patient.

West starts with a simple 2NT call, a general game try. East can accept, having a maximum balanced hand for his 2♠ raise. Accordingly, he converts to cuebidding, in case 2NT was actually a cuebid. East cuebids 3♣, showing a club control.

This helps West, who can now cuebid 3◊ to show a diamond control. East contributes 3♡. West now bids 4◊, showing the double control in diamonds and making clear that slam is the focus. This clarifies retroactively for East that the 2NT call was meant to show a lack of two top trumps, but this is no surprise.

Back to East. He has two potentially useful features that he has been unable to show so far, namely two of the top spades and the heart doubleton. Uncertain what to do, but realizing the value of his hand, he should simply cuebid 4♡, Last Train.

With the same hand and the diamond queen, he would have opened 1NT, unless he held a singleton heart.

With the ideal hand

♠ A Q 5 4   ♡ 8   ◊ 9 3 2   ♣ A K 5 4 2

he would have made a Picture Splinter after 2NT.

With a flawed hand, like

♠ A Q 5 4   ♡ 8   ◊ Q 9 3   ♣ A 5 4 3 2

he would have made a delayed splinter after 3◇. Hence, we expect him not to have a singleton heart, but rather to have an honor control in hearts. This forces his 4♡ Last Train call to feature something like what he actually holds.

Ultimately, West must use judgment, but he will be much better placed to make an educated guess now than after the actual auction.

On these hands from the 2004 World Bridge Olympiad, very few pairs reached a solid slam.

WEST	EAST
♠ A K 9 5 2	♠ Q 7 3
♡ Q 9 8	♡ A K J 4 2
◇ K 4	◇ A 8 5 2
♣ 10 5 4	♣ 2

At both tables in the Vugraph match, West opened 1♠, East bid 2♡ and West raised to 3♡. East then tried 3♠ and West signed off in 4♡. The consensus auction:

WEST	EAST
1♠	2♡
3♡	3♠
4♡	pass

The 'easy' route to 6♡ is for West to cooperate and cuebid 4◇. Given the bypass of 3NT, East is not entitled to assume West has any extra strength. However, knowing West has little to no club wastage and a diamond control should be sufficient for East to try for slam.

Note one potential pitfall on this auction: 3♠ is clearly a cuebid. It does not shift us back and forth between the majors. Hearts is agreed and that decision does not change.

Reaching only a small slam can be costly in high-level events, as happened to many teams on this, our final deal, from the 2004 World Bridge Olympiad (hands rotated):

WEST	EAST
♠ 5 2	♠ A J 10 3
♡ A Q 9 6 2	♡ K J 10
◇ K Q 6	◇ A
♣ K Q 3	♣ A 8 6 5 4

One of the few teams to reach the grand did so using what to us seems a simple and familiar maneuver. After 1♡-2♣, West rebid 2◊. This slight misdescription is justified for three reasons. First, rebidding 2NT without a spade stopper would not be a violation, but is not desirable. Second, it enables West to cuebid diamonds later to show his two diamond honors (and enables East to complete the diamond picture, for that matter). Third, it facilitates a cheaper establishment of hearts as trumps. After 2◊ from West, East can bid 2♡ to set trumps, saving a world of space.

The grand slam is reached as follows:

WEST	EAST
1♡	2♣
2◊[1]	2♡
3♣[2]	3◊[3]
4♣[4]	5◊[5]
6♣[6]	7♡

1. Tactical.
2. No spade control, good trumps, one top club honor.
3. One top diamond honor, plus spades under control.
4. Second top club honor, non-serious contextually (actually, tactical).
5. RKCB, diamonds focused.
6. Two contextual 'keycards', plus the diamond queen.

The auction may need more explanation as to the 5◊ call from East. When East showed a top diamond honor, he denied shortness, so Exclusion RKCB for diamonds is not possible. As usual, when shortness can be ruled out, the five-level call is RKCB, with the keycards being shifted to focus on the asking suit.

West's 4♣ call sets up this nice auction. Realizing that it was more important to show two top club honors than general slam interest, he paints a picture for East, who can easily visualize twelve tricks. The best source for extra strength is in diamonds. Hence, the 5◊ call. This is a great example of a hand where a keycard shift is not used to seek help for one's own suit, but rather as a type of asking bid, to check on top honors in partner's suit.